EVENTS THAT CHANGED THE WORLD

1820–1840

=The Nineteenth Century=

Jennifer Bussey, *Book Editor*

Bruce Glassman, *Vice President*
Bonnie Szumski, *Publisher*
Helen Cothran, *Managing Editor*

GREENHAVEN PRESS
An imprint of Thomson Gale, a part of The Thomson Corporation

Detroit • New York • San Francisco • San Diego • New Haven, Conn.
Waterville, Maine • London • Munich

© 2005 Thomson Gale, a part of The Thomson Corporation.

Thomson and Star Logo are trademarks and Gale and Greenhaven Press are registered trademarks used herein under license.

For more information, contact
Greenhaven Press
27500 Drake Rd.
Farmington Hills, MI 48331-3535
Or you can visit our Internet site at http://www.gale.com

ALL RIGHTS RESERVED.
No part of this work covered by the copyright hereon may be reproduced or used in any form or by any means—graphic, electronic, or mechanical, including photocopying, recording, taping, Web distribution or information storage retrieval systems—without the written permission of the publisher.

Every effort has been made to trace the owners of copyrighted material.

Cover credit: © Mary Evans Picture Library
Library of Congress, 51, 77
Prints Old and Rare, 103

LIBRARY OF CONGRESS CATALOGING-IN-PUBLICATION DATA

1820–1840 / Jennifer Bussey, book editor.
   p. cm. — (Events that changed the world)
Includes bibliographical references and index.
ISBN 0-7377-2031-X (alk. paper)
   1. History, Modern—19th century. 2. Inventions—History—19th century.
I. Bussey, Jennifer. II. Series.
D358.A125 2005
909.81—dc22   2004052393

Printed in the United States of America

CONTENTS

Foreword 7

Introduction 10

Event 1: Michael Faraday Discovers Electromagnetic Rotation: September 1821

1. **Michael Faraday's Discoveries Led to the Practical Application of Electricity**
   by Keith J. Laidler 14
   The great physicist's discovery of electromagnetic rotation and subsequent breakthroughs led to enormous advances in science and technology.

Event 2: Mexico Wins Independence from Spain: September 27, 1821

1. **Mexico's Long Fight for Independence**
   by Burton Kirkwood 21
   After years of dissension and fighting, Mexico finally won its independence from Spain. This hard-won opportunity, however, brought challenges to both Mexico and Spain.

Event 3: Liberia Is Founded as a Colony: January 1822

1. **Liberia: American Blacks' Attempts at a Colony**
   by John H. Smyth 28
   While Liberia offered great opportunities to African Americans, thriving there required tenacity, self-sufficiency, and luck.

Event 4: The Monroe Doctrine: December 2, 1823

1. **The Monroe Doctrine Establishes America's Political and Economic Independence from Europe**
   by Richard W. Leopold — 38
   Perceived threats from abroad, coupled with America's growing nationalism, prompted the Monroe Doctrine.

2. **The United States Opposes European Intervention in the Western Hemisphere**
   by James Monroe — 49
   President Monroe's doctrine of nonintervention was a bold statement of sovereignty intended to free America from European political maneuvers and land-grabbing.

Event 5: The Decembrist Uprising: December 14, 1825

1. **The Decembrist Revolt Signals the Start of Russia's Revolutionary History**
   by Anatole G. Mazour — 55
   Frustrated by lack of social reform, a group of aristocratic Russians attempted to overthrow the czar. Although their effort failed, their revolutionary spirit took hold among the Russian people.

Event 6: The Nat Turner Uprising: August 21–22, 1831

1. **Panic After the Nat Turner Uprising Begins to Change Racial Attitudes Toward Slavery**
   by Herbert Aptheker — 61
   In the wake of the horrific events of the Nat Turner slave uprising, southerners reacted with shock, panic, and horror. The fear that more such

massacres were being planned swept the southern states.

2. **Turner's Account of the Uprising**
   by Nat Turner   73
   The mastermind and leader of the bloody revolt, Nat Turner, gave his full confession while in prison awaiting execution. He expresses no remorse as he explains the religious, moral, and vindictive motivations for the killings.

Event 7: The Treaty of London: May 7, 1832

1. **Greek Nationalism Is Finally Rewarded with Independence**
   by Augustus Oakes and R.B. Mowat   84
   After years of growing nationalism, Greece was on the brink of revolution. With the help of Great Britain, France, and Russia, Greek independence was secured from Turkey.

Event 8: The Coronation of Queen Victoria: June 28, 1838

1. **The Legacy of Queen Victoria's Reign**
   by Lynne Vallone   97
   Victoria's ascension to the throne had an important and unexpected impact on the British Empire. Her influence was so strong that the era is known by her name, the Victorian age.

2. **Firsthand Accounts of the Coronation Ceremony**
   by Christopher Hibbert   106
   To outsiders, Victoria's coronation must have seemed austere and formal, but to those who participated, the event was emotional and nerve-wracking.

Event 9: The Underground Railroad Is Officially Established: 1838

1. The Underground Railroad Undermined Slavery
by Albert Bushnell Hart   113
Once escaped slaves survived the trials of making their way through the South to the free states in the North, the Underground Railroad and abolitionists assisted them in their flight to Canada.

2. Preface to Records of the Underground Railroad
by William Still   118
In his introductory remarks to records kept regarding the Underground Railroad, Still considers the significance of the slaves' willingness to escape bondage and the bravery of the men and women who made escape routes possible.

Event 10: Charles Goodyear Discovers the Process of Rubber Vulcanization: 1839

1. Goodyear's Accomplishment Changes Industry and Everyday Life
by Charles Slack   123
After years of hard work and sacrifice, Goodyear discovered the process of rubber vulcanization. The discovery changed industry and daily life, but others disputed Goodyear's patent rights.

Chronology	131
For Further Research	135
Index	138

FOREWORD

In 1543 a Polish astronomer named Nicolaus Copernicus published a book entitled *De revolutionibus orbium coelestium* in which he theorized that Earth revolved around the Sun. In 1688, during the Glorious Revolution, Dutch prince William of Orange invaded England and overthrew King James II. In 1922 Irish author James Joyce's novel *Ulysses*, which describes one day in Dublin, was published.

Although these events are seemingly unrelated, occurring in different nations and in different centuries, they all share the distinction of having changed the world. Although Copernicus's book had a relatively minor impact at the time of its publication, it eventually had a momentous influence. The Copernican system provided a foundation on which future scientists could develop an accurate understanding of the solar system. Perhaps more importantly, it required humanity to contemplate the possibility that Earth, far from occupying a special place at the center of creation, was merely one planet in a vast universe. In doing so, it forced a reevaluation of the Christian cosmology that had served as the foundation of Western culture. As professor Thomas S. Kuhn writes, "The drama of Christian life and the morality that had been made dependent upon it would not readily adapt to a universe in which the earth was just one of a number of planets."

Like the Copernican revolution, the Glorious Revolution of 1688–1689 had a profound influence on the future of Western societies. By deposing James II, William and his wife, Mary, ended the Stuart dynasty, a series of monarchs who had favored the Catholic Church and had limited the power of Parliament for decades. Under William and Mary, Parliament passed the Bill of Rights, which established the legislative supremacy of Parliament and barred Roman Catholics from the throne. These actions initiated the gradual process by which the power of the government of England shifted from the monarchy to Parliament, establishing a democratic system that would be copied, with some variations, by the United States and other democratic societies worldwide.

Whereas the Glorious Revolution had a major impact in the political sphere, the publication of Joyce's novel *Ulysses* represented a revolution in literature. In an effort to capture the sense of chaos and discontinuity that permeated the culture in the wake of World War I, Joyce did away with the use of straightforward narrative that had dominated fiction up to that time. The novel, whose structure mirrors that of Homer's *Odyssey*, combines realistic descriptions of events with passages that convey the characters' inner experience by means of a technique known as stream of consciousness, in which the characters' thoughts and feelings are presented without regard to logic or narrative order. Due to its departure from the traditional modes of fiction, *Ulysses* is often described as one of the seminal works of modernist literature. As stated by Pennsylvania State University professor Michael H. Begnal, "*Ulysses* is the novel that changed the direction of 20th-century fiction written in English."

Copernicus's theory of a sun-centered solar system, the Glorious Revolution, and James Joyce's *Ulysses* are just three examples of time-bound events that have had far-reaching effects—for better or worse—on the progress of human societies worldwide. History is made up of an inexhaustible list of such events. In the twentieth century alone, for example, one can isolate any number of world-shattering moments: the first performance of Igor Stravinsky's ballet *The Rites of Spring* in 1913; Japan's attack on Pearl Harbor on December 7, 1941; the launch of the satellite *Sputnik* on October 4, 1957. These events variously influenced the culture, society, and political configuration of the twentieth century.

Greenhaven Press's Events That Changed the World series is designed to help readers learn about world history by examining seemingly random events that have had the greatest influence on the development of cultures, societies, and governments throughout the ages. The series is divided into sets of several anthologies, with each set covering a period of one hundred years. Each volume begins with an introduction that provides essential context on the time period being covered. Then, the major events of the era are covered by means of primary and secondary sources. Primary sources include firsthand accounts, speeches, correspondence, and other materials that bring history alive. Secondary sources analyze the profound effects the events had on the world. Each reading is preceded by an introduction that puts it in context and emphasizes the event's importance in the ongoing evolution of world history. Additional features add to the value of the series: An annotated table of contents and an index allow readers to quickly locate material of interest. A chronology provides an easy reference for contextual information. And a bibliography offers opportunities for further exploration. All of these features help to make the Events That Changed the World series a valuable resource for readers interested in the major events that have shaped the course of humanity.

INTRODUCTION

The first half of the nineteenth century was a period of worldwide change. The discovery of electromagnetic induction by British physicist Michael Faraday in 1821 began a new era of scientific and technological advances; the opening of the Erie Canal in 1825 and the Baltimore and Ohio Railroad in 1829 transformed the economy and settlement of the United States; and the coronation of Queen Victoria in 1837 marked the beginning of a new political era in England. Political change proved to be the hallmark of the decades 1820–1840, in part because the removal of Napoléon I from power in 1815 had galvanized democratic and nationalistic reform movements across Europe and in far-flung European colonies. Unlike Victoria's orderly, peaceful succession, however, most of the era's political change involved conflict, from internal demands for reform to widespread struggles for independence against foreign domination to violent revolution.

The End of European Influence in the Americas

Spain and Portugal, two of Europe's major colonial powers, simultaneously faced internal revolts and splintering of their empires between 1820 and 1840. In 1820 a dissident faction of military units led by Colonel Rafael de Reigo successfully pressured Spanish king Ferdinand VII into restoring the liberal French constitution of 1812. More garrisons rallied to the liberal cause and the monarchy teetered, but Ferdinand managed to put down the rebellion in 1823 with the help of French troops. That was the beginning of decades of violent civil unrest in Spain, as royalists battled republicans and general confusion, lawlessness, and banditry prevailed. Spain's colonies took advantage of the military and administrative chaos: By 1840 every Spanish possession in the Americas, including Mexico, most of Central and South America, and the Caribbean except for Cuba and Puerto Rico, had won independence. (Independence rarely meant stability, however; Mexico, for example, would struggle under at least fifty different governing regimes in the thirty-five years following independence in 1821.)

A similar revolt in Portugal in 1820 ousted the existing British regency and created a shaky constitutional monarchy. For the next two decades, supporters of the monarchy known as absolutists, backed by the aristocracy and the peasantry, battled the liberals of the large cities and middle class, who promoted constitutional reform and representative government. Eventually the two sides reached a constitutional compromise and peace was restored in 1838, but by that time Portugal's South American colony, Brazil, had won its independence. Without an outpost in the Americas, Portugal soon turned to Africa, as did Belgium after throwing off Dutch rule in 1830, and a new era of largely destructive African colonization began.

European Involvement in the Greek War of Independence

All of the great powers of Europe were either directly or indirectly involved in one revolutionary movement of the 1820–1840 era: the Greek war of independence. Greece had been under the yoke of the Ottoman Empire, centered in Turkey, for nearly four hundred years, since the fall of Constantinople in 1453. Under harsh Turkish oppression, the Greeks had no recent tradition of self-rule or self-sufficiency, but democratic ideals formed the core of ancient Greek civilization and nationalistic sentiment, beyond simple hatred of the non-Christian Turks, was still a strong aspect of the Greek character. In 1821 Greek revolutionaries in the Peloponnese, backed by the church and wealthy merchant class, revolted against the decadent and generally declining Ottoman sultanate, beginning a bloody, nine-year conflict marked by extraordinary cruelty and massacres on both sides.

The Greek war of independence was a war of gradual liberation. The revolutionaries gained control of the Peloponnese within a year, but factional rivalries prevented them from developing unified objectives and a sound strategy elsewhere, and internal disagreements twice led to civil war in the midst of the conflict, the most serious in 1824. The Turkish sultan took advantage of this weakness and, with allied Egyptian naval forces, recaptured key Peloponnesian cities all the way to Athens and the Athenian acropolis in 1826, threatening the entire revolution.

At that point, the European powers—England, France, Austria, and Russia—intervened, motivated more by rivalries of their own than by support for the Greek cause. As historian C.W. Crawley notes:

> In a sense the mutual suspicion of the Powers was the Greeks' best security: no one of them was concerned to make Greece an independent State . . . but each was driven in that direction by the fear of allowing the other an excuse for further [unilateral] interference. The native Greeks cared little for their diplomatic status so long as the Turks were excluded from their midst; the interests of the Powers more than the enthusiasm of the people eventually made Greece into an independent kingdom.[1]

At first the powers offered to mediate the formation of an autonomous Greek state. When the Turks refused a cease-fire, a combined British, French, and Russian fleet destroyed the Egyptian fleet at Navarino in 1827, crippling Ottoman forces, and the conflict became even more complicated. The Turks and Russians went to war in Bulgaria and the Caucasus as the Ottomans continued to fight the Greeks. Ultimately the Turks were forced to sue for peace in both conflicts: Negotiated settlements in 1828 and 1829 granted Greece the status of independent monarchical state under the protection of the European powers and severely, and permanently, limited Ottoman influence in the Balkans and Mediterranean.

A Sign of Political Change to Come

Even the most notable failed uprising of the era, the Decembrist Uprising of 1825 in Russia, signaled political change by striking the first significant blow against czarist rule. Already a multinational and multireligious state by 1800, Russia had become even larger and more diverse in the early nineteenth century. Finland was annexed from Sweden in 1809, Bessarabia from Turkey in 1812, and central Poland, including Warsaw, in 1815. (The lands of the Caucasus Mountains, including Georgia, Armenia, and Azerbaijan, would be incorporated by 1859.)

Russian patriotism had been boosted by the defeat of French emperor Napoléon I, whose army's ruinous march to Moscow and famous retreat were depicted by Leo Tolstoy in his epic *War and Peace*. But Russian officers and conscripted commoners alike returned from their eye-opening experiences in the Napoleonic Wars in western Europe to disappointing, repressive conditions at home. After the death of Czar Alexander I in 1825, his brother Nicholas

I was immediately faced with a conspiracy to remove him from power. The revolutionaries, who became known as the Decembrists (after the month the plot was launched), were a mixed group of intellectuals, idealistic military officers, and aristocrats. Though essentially disorganized and lacking public support, they incited the soldiers of some imperial guards to revolt. The uprising, however, was summarily crushed, its leaders either hanged or exiled. But change was coming, just the same. The Decembrist Uprising ignited a revolutionary movement that would dominate Russian history for the next century.

British historian Emma Rothschild characterizes the early nineteenth century as an "age of insubordination,"[2] leading to a changed, postrevolutionary world in which commerce and competition for markets, not national sovereignty, was the basis of both political stability, political alliances, and political disruption. This important historical transition occurred largely in the brief period between 1820 and 1840. *Events That Changed the World: 1820–1840* examines the key events of this period to help readers understand not only immediate political and social changes but also their profound effects in the decades that followed.

Notes

1. C.W. Crawley, *The Question of Greek Independence: A Study of British Policy in the Near East, 1821–1833*. Cambridge, England: Cambridge University Press, 1930, p. 77.
2. Emma Rothschild, "The Age of Insubordination," *Foreign Policy*, Summer 2000, p. 46.

EVENT 1

Michael Faraday Discovers Electromagnetic Rotation: September 1821

Michael Faraday's Discoveries Led to the Practical Application of Electricity

by Keith J. Laidler

Michael Faraday (1791–1867), one of the great scientific minds of the nineteenth century, was an English physicist and chemist whose intense curiosity and unparalleled skill in experimentation led to his discovery of electromagnetic rotation and, later, electromagnetic induction. These discoveries proved that electrical energy can be converted to mechanical energy and vice versa. Faraday's research paved the way for the inventions of the electric motor, generator, and transformer. In his later career, he also made important contributions to the field of electrochemistry. The endless applications and possibilities of these technologies are a major factor in the development of industrial society.

In the following selection, science historian Keith J. Laidler describes Faraday's inspirations and methods as well as the significance and consequences of his work. Laidler, professor emeritus of chemistry at the University of Ottawa, is the author of *Energy and the Unexpected* and numerous scholarly books on physical and theoretical chemistry.

Keith J. Laidler, *To Light Such a Candle: Chapters in the History of Science and Technology.* Oxford, UK: Oxford University Press, 1998. Copyright © 1998 by Keith Laidler. Reproduced by permission.

The career of Michael Faraday provides us with an excellent example of how pure research, done as a result of scientific curiosity and with little regard for any possible applications, may nevertheless have far-reaching practical consequences. In some of his work Faraday did show interest in practical matters, but in much of it, particularly that on electricity and magnetism, he was mainly motivated by curiosity and a desire to formulate a theory of the behaviour of electric currents and of magnets.

Modern society is highly dependent on electric power, used for heating, lighting, and communication. The great transformation that has occurred since the early nineteenth century was greatly influenced by Michael Faraday's researches. In 1821 he was the first person to convert the energy of an electrical current into mechanical energy. Even more important, his discovery of electromagnetic induction in 1831 led to the efficient conversion of mechanical energy into electrical energy, and directly led to the vast modern electrical industry in which electricity is distributed on a large scale throughout the world. Also, and again of great importance, Faraday's unconventional ideas about electric and magnetic fields led James Clerk Maxwell to formulate his great theory of electromagnetism, and to recognize that light is a form of electromagnetic radiation. The development of radio techniques, with all their consequences, was soon to follow the publication of Maxwell's ideas. . . .

Faraday's Expertise as a Physicist

At first Faraday's main work at the Royal Institution was in chemistry. By 1820 he had established a reputation as an analytical chemist, and from this work he was able to supplement his modest salary and also contribute to the support of the Royal Institution itself, which was not well endowed. Some of Faraday's chemical work was concerned with clays, and some was on metal alloys; he prepared several novel varieties of steel, from some of which he fabricated razors for himself and his friends. Occasionally Faraday appeared in court as an expert witness. One of these cases related to oil, and Faraday was led to investigate the properties of oils and gases which were beginning to be used for public heating and lighting. It was as a result of these studies that Faraday discovered benzene in 1825. Since this compound is the prototype of a vast number of organic compounds, this was a discovery of great importance. He also discovered a number of other important chemical compounds. One of these was the first recorded example of what is now called a clathrate compound—it was a compound in which a chlorine molecule is buried inside a group of water molecules. (*Clathri* is the Latin for a lattice or trellis, and the water molecules form a kind of trellis round the inner molecule.) An example of a clathrate compound is found in permafrost, where water molecules trap methane (CH^4) molecules. Faraday was the first to liquefy a number of gases, such as ammonia and carbon dioxide.

In 1820, soon after André Marie Ampère (a French physicist) had presented his interpretation of Hans Christian Oersted's [Danish physicist who showed how an electric current in a wire could move a compass needle] result, Faraday's friend Richard Phillips, an editor of the *Philosophical Magazine*, persuaded him to look into the subject of electromagnetism. Like other editors of scientific journals, Phillips had been inundated with papers on the subject. Faraday accepted Phillips's suggestion rather reluctantly, as he considered that his skills were confined to chemistry, and his interests had been far from electromagnetism. Eventually he agreed to look into the work of Oersted and the later work of Ampère, and posterity must be grateful to Phillips for his gentle but persistent prodding.

Faraday's Discovery About Electrical Energy

Faraday at once repeated Oersted's experiments, and he noticed that when a small magnetic needle was moved round a wire carrying a current, one of the poles turned in a circle. He then speculated that a single magnetic pole, if it could exist, would move continuously around a wire as long as the current flowed. This led him to perform an experiment of great simplicity and also of great importance. In 1821 he attached a magnet upright to the bottom of a deep basin, and then filled the basin with mercury so that only the pole of the magnet was above the surface. A wire free to move was attached above the bowl and dipped into the mercury. When Faraday passed a current through the wire and the magnet, the wire continuously rotated around the magnet. In an adaptation of the experiment, he caused the magnet to rotate around the wire. He also succeeded in rotating a wire by use of the magnetism of the earth. The great importance of these simple demonstrations is that electrical energy was being converted into mechanical energy for the first time. To Faraday the results implied that there were circular lines of force round the current-carrying wire, and he accepted this as a simple experimental fact. Almost everyone else concluded that the force could not be simple, but must be explained in some way in terms of central forces. ...

Faraday Discovers Electromagnetic Induction

In 1831 Michael Faraday made one of his most famous discoveries, electromagnetic induction. It is often said that this discovery led to the invention of electric motors, but it is much more likely that they came directly from the work on electromagnets. ...

Faraday frequently experimented with the idea that a wire bearing a current might induce a current in a nearby wire. Until 29 August 1831, however, he always failed to find any effect. On that day he wound one side of a soft-iron ring with insulated wire, and arranged a secondary winding, connected to a galvanometer, around the other side. At first he thought that the experiment was again a failure. He noticed, however, that when he turned off the electric current in the primary coil, believing the experiment to have failed, the galvanometer revealed a sudden short flow in the secondary circuit. Closer investigation showed that a continuous current in the primary circuit had no effect; it was only when the current was started or stopped that there was an effect on the galvanometer. Joseph Henry later claimed that he had discovered electromagnetic induction at the same time as Faraday, and quite independently; there is no reason to doubt this, but Henry had not published his results.

Soon after his discovery of electromagnetic induction in 1831, Faraday demonstrated that if he pushed a magnet into a coil of wire, a transient current was produced. A current was generated in the opposite direction when the magnet was withdrawn. No current passed when the magnet was stationary; to generate a current the magnet had to be moved in relation to the coil.

The important point is that electromagnetic induction only occurs if there is a change in an electric current, which means that there is a change in the magnetism. Oersted and Ampère had shown that a steady electric current produces a magnetic field, and Faraday and his contemporaries thought at first that if a wire were placed near to a magnet, an electric current would be generated. Attempts to demonstrate this were, however, unsuccessful, and it was first believed that success might be achieved if a stronger magnetic field were employed. Being wise after the event we can see today that such a result would be impossible. We are now aware—which Faraday was not at the time—of the necessity for energy to be conserved. If a stationary magnet (either a permanent magnet or an electromagnet) were to induce an electric current in a nearby wire we would be getting something for nothing—where would the energy come from? We think so much in terms of energy today that it is hard to realize that before the middle of the nineteenth century the word energy was hardly ever used, and that even the most competent scientific investigators were unaware of its great importance. In addition, even Faraday was only just beginning to realize that an electric current involves a movement of electric charge. Oersted had discovered that a steady current of electricity would affect a magnet; however, we now know that an electric current involves a moving electric charge, and that energy (from a battery, for example) is being used up in creating it. It had also been found by Arago and Sturgeon that an electric current (a moving electric charge) in a coiled wire would produce a magnet. Thus to produce an electric current we need some change in a magnetic field—this can be produced by moving a permanent magnet (which uses up energy), or by switching on or off the current in a solenoid. A stationary magnet cannot be expected to give rise to electromagnetic induction, because there is no source of energy.

Faraday's Discoveries Built On Each Other

Faraday's 1821 discovery of electromagnetic rotation had shown that electrical energy could be converted into motion. In 1831 he succeeded in converting mechanical motion into electricity. He rotated a copper disc between the poles of a magnet, and found that a steady current flowed from the centre of the disc to its edge. This achievement encouraged Faraday to carry out the further researches, particularly those on electrolysis, which were to lead to the announcement in 1838 of his general theory of electric and magnetic fields. . . .

Faraday worked unrelentingly for many years. He and his wife lived in an apartment at the Royal Institution, so that his laboratory was close at hand. His extensive notebooks show that he wasted no time, and worked long hours six days a week; his religion required Sundays to be days of rest, but he took no others. It was not uncommon for him to work in his laboratory from nine in the morning to eleven at night, with only short breaks. He made all his own extensive notes on his experimental results, and had no help in writing the 450 articles he published, and the several books he wrote. . . .

Faraday's Scientific Legacy

Some idea of Michael Faraday's scientific eminence is gained by a speculation as to how many Nobel Prizes he would have received if there had been such prizes in his time. The first Nobel Prizes were awarded in 1901, and by now we have a good idea of the criteria that are used in awarding them: we can therefore make a reasonable guess as to how Faraday would have fared if the Prizes had been awarded earlier. So far no one has won more than two Nobel Prizes, but it seems likely that Faraday would have won six. He would surely have got a Nobel Prize for chemistry for his discovery of benzene (1825), the prototype of a vast number of organic compounds. It is hard to see how he could have been overlooked for Nobel Prizes for physics for his discovery of electromagnetic rotation (1821), his discovery of electromagnetic induction (1830), his laws of electrolysis (1834), his work on dielectrics (1837), and his discovery of paramagnetism and diamagnetism (1845).

It is hard to think of anyone else who would have deserved so many Nobel Prizes. Isaac Newton might have won two, for his mechanics and his optics, and possibly a third (shared with Gottfried Wilhelm Leibnitz) for his calculus. James Clerk Maxwell would probably have won two, for his distribution of molecular speeds and his theory of electromagnetic radiation. Albert Einstein did win one Prize, for his work on the quantum theory, but surely should have had another one for his work on relativity. The suggestion that Faraday deserved six prizes puts him in a class by himself.

Faraday's researches into electricity and magnetism fall clearly into the category of pure science or basic research. They were motivated mainly by his curiosity about the nature of electricity and magnetism, and only to a small extent by his desire to make practical use of electricity. His discoveries nevertheless had far-reaching practical implications.

It is important not to exaggerate these, as is often done. It is sometimes said, for example, that the electric motor owes its origin to Faraday's work, but this is not the case. The work of William

Sturgeon and Joseph Henry on electromagnets, done before Faraday discovered electromagnetic induction, had more to do with the development of electric motors.

Practical Applications of Faraday's Work

It is, on the other hand, reasonable to claim that it was Faraday's work on electromagnetic induction (1831) that led to the *dynamo*, or rotary electric generator. The principle of such devices is that coils of wire are moved relative to the field of a magnet, so that an electric current is produced; a generator, in fact, is an electric motor operated in reverse. The first to construct an electric generator seems to have been the instrument maker Hyppolyte Pixii (1808–1835), who exhibited one to the Académie des Sciences in Paris in 1832. A permanent horseshoe magnet was rotated relative to a wire coil, and in later devices coils were rotated relative to magnets. Soon permanent magnets were replaced by electromagnets activated by batteries. In 1866 CF Varley (1823–1883) discovered and patented the principle of self-excitation, in which the electromagnets are activated by the electricity produced by the generator itself. By that time it had been realized that electromagnets having soft-iron cores possessed enough residual magnetism to provide the magnetic field necessary to initiate the output from a generator. At about the same time Werner von Siemens (1816–1892) demonstrated similar devices to the Berlin Academy of Sciences, and it was he who invented the word dynamo.

It is correct to credit Faraday with producing the prototype of the electrical transformer. If in his experiments of 1831 he had continuously reversed the direction of the current in coil A, he would have observed an alternating current in coil B; that is, the current in coil B would have continually changed its direction. Today most of the electric power that is transmitted from one place to another is sent not as a steady, or direct, current, but as an alternating current. In North America alternating current usually changes its direction sixty times a second, which we call sixty cycles a second, or sixty hertz; in Britain and elsewhere the alternating current is at fifty cycles a second. Such alternating current is directly produced by rotary generators, and is readily converted from one voltage to another by the use of a transformer based on Faraday's iron ring.

EVENT 2

Mexico Wins Independence from Spain: September 27, 1821

Mexico's Long Fight for Independence

by Burton Kirkwood

After three hundred years of Spanish colonization, Mexico (then called New Spain) won its independence in 1821 after almost fifteen years of armed resistance. The Mexicans were determined to rule themselves and keep their money and resources to build their own country, but they soon discovered that self-rule was extremely challenging. A string of military strongmen proved unable to establish the political and economic stability Mexico needed, and internal turmoil continued for decades.

In the following article Burton Kirkwood describes the events and sentiments leading up to Mexico's final push for independence. He also reviews the uncertainty and turmoil in Mexico as its people faced the daunting task of creating a sustainable government, economy, and society. Kirkwood is an associate professor of history at the University of Evansville in Indiana, where he also serves as the director of the World Cultures Sequence.

Mexico's independence from Spain, which began in the early nineteenth century, was not revolutionary. The process reflected the conservative interests of the landed elite and their response to European events rather than specific actions in Mexico; in other words, the process of breaking away from

---

Burton Kirkwood, *The History of Mexico*. Westport, CT: Greenwood Press, 2000. Copyright © 2000 by Burton Kirkwood. All rights reserved. Reproduced by permission.

Spain was more reactionary than proactive. The royal Spanish government's enactment of the Bourbon reforms in the second half of the eighteenth century exacerbated social, economic, and political conditions within Mexico. With the French seizure of Spain in 1808, the imposition of Joseph Bonaparte on the throne, and the creation of the Cádiz junta [a group of military rulers] Mexico exploded into crisis. The instability revealed acute social divisions within Mexico. The upper classes sought to establish an autonomous government that would represent their interests, and the lower classes struggled against the dominance of the local elites.

The multiple reforms discussed in Mexico revealed the disparities between the various classes struggling to preserve their interests. Yet some common complaints were shared by the diverse groups. For example, the growing inability of Spain to effectively govern Mexico provoked widespread discontent. Also, a sense of *Mexicanidad* (an identity with things Mexican) fostered an attitude that rejected the long-established idea that somehow things European were superior. These conditions gave rise to demands for a more extensive role for Mexicans within the governing infrastructure. When French soldiers seized Spain, the discussion about independence found a willing audience.

Mexico's Financial Relationship with Spain

As the Spanish Crown struggled for its own preservation, it looked to its colonies for assistance, primarily in the form of money to pay its mounting expenses. As Mexicans were asked to provide more financial support to Spain, the question of their relationship to the Crown became more intangible. Specifically, their sense of loyalty was tested as the demands from Spain increased.

At the end of the eighteenth century Mexico was the richest of Spain's colonies in the New World. Of the income generated by its colonies, more than 60 percent came from Mexico. As John Lynch [contributor to *The Independence of Latin America*] has pointed out, this put Mexico in a new situation—Spain depended on the colony more than Mexico relied on Spain. Of course the demands for more money heightened discontent in Mexico. Throughout its history money had been raised by "voluntary" contributions, often paid by the wealthiest within Mexico who used the contributions to ensure advancement and access to power. With the mounting instability in Europe, Spain needed more money than voluntary contributions could provide. Rising taxes affected virtually all sectors of the population, providing a device that cut across class lines—everyone could identify with this complaint, regardless of social position.

The elite grew angry when the Crown made it increasingly difficult to establish the conditions whereby the property of a family stayed intact and passed to the next generation. In Mexico this policy was institutionalized in the procedure known as the entail *(mayorazgo)*. Under this system an elite family could ensure the preservation of its property as well as the obtainment of noble distinction. As the crisis grew in Europe, the Crown raised the costs for obtaining an entail. Some protested the exorbitant costs, while others simply abandoned the idea of establishing a *mayorazgo*.

Not only did the elites grow angry, but soon the Crown's demands affected artisans and the Church itself. Spain demanded loans from various guilds in Mexico. Three principal functions of the guilds were to provide funds to assist disabled workers, to support families who had lost members within the guilds, and to invest money in artisans or merchants to help expand the colonial economy. The last function was probably the most important because this money helped drive the capital-poor economy of the colony. However, the Crown saw the funds held by the guilds as a source of income.

The Crown's miscalculations continued when the monarchy introduced the Royal Law of Consolidation in the winter of 1804. The law authorized the government to seize Church lands that would then be auctioned off, as well as to seize money lent out to individuals, in order to meet the rising expenditures incurred in Europe. Just as it had with the guilds, this move against the Church threatened to weaken the colonial economy by reducing money available for internal loans. By the end of the eighteenth century the Church was the largest money lender in Mexico; in fact, in the area around Guadalajara it loaned as much as 70 percent of the funds for commercial projects. Consequently "capital rather than property was the principal wealth of the Mexican Church." Opposition to the Royal Law of Consolidation was strong, but rather than invoke the established practice of ignoring royal decrees, the viceroy José de Iturrigaray, operating in the reformist spirit of the Bourbon kings, implemented the policy.

The impact of the decree reached all sectors of Mexico even though it remained in effect for only four years. Most affected were small landholders and businessmen who operated with

Church loans. Faced with the immediacy of the royal decree, the Church demanded immediate payment of all loans. Those who could not make the payment had to sell their holdings at an inopportune time—it became a buyers' market, and many property holders suffered. One of the landholders affected by the decree was the father of a parish priest, Father Miguel Hidalgo y Costilla.

Conflict Among Mexican People

The Crown's colonial economic demands furthered the colonists' dissatisfaction developed toward Spain. By the nineteenth century in Mexico there emerged the sentiment that Mexicans had a nearly equal status with people from the Iberian peninsula. Increasingly there could be heard the cry favoring the monarchy but opposing the continuation of bad government. The German traveler and scientist Alexander von Humboldt visited Mexico at the beginning of the nineteenth century and noted the social disparities, concluding that conditions were ripe for an "explosion of social conflict."

The seizure of Spain by the French, and Ferdinand VII's abdication of the throne in 1808, resulted in the Creoles [those born in Mexico] demanding autonomy. This was presented to Viceroy Iturrigaray in July 1808. The Creole demands were conservative, but for Peninsulares [those born in Spain] any relationship between the viceroy and Creoles suggested a sympathetic view toward Creole interests. The conservative objective of the proposal was revealed when elite Creoles asked the viceroy to assume leadership of a junta (a temporary, provisional governing body) made up of representatives of the principal cities in Mexico. Moreover, the conservative direction was underscored by the proclamation that the junta existed due to the absence of royal leadership. The implicit assumption was that the junta would step down when the king was restored to the throne. Finally, what was proposed in Mexico was being duplicated in Spain, where juntas were established during the uncertainty of foreign rule.

Although precedent existed for such a call, the proposal sparked division and outrage as the Peninsulares feared the loss of their interests under a Creole-led junta. Rather than call the junta, Viceroy Iturrigaray convoked an assembly of representatives from Mexico City. The viceroy's lack of decisiveness fed the fears of the Peninsulares that the government was poorly managed and in need of competent leadership. A contentious atmosphere dominated the meeting, and divisions developed as to who was being represented—Creoles or Peninsulares. Also, arguments arose whether Mexico would recognize the Seville junta in Spain or establish a junta in New Spain acting in the name of Ferdinand VII. Motivated by this acrimonious debate, the Peninsulares decided to act.

First Violent Outbreak

Early on September 16, 1808, the Peninsulares, led by Gabriel de Yermo (a wealthy plantation owner), initiated a coup by seizing Iturrigaray and replacing him with Pedro de Garibay. The Peninsulares believed they acted in a manner loyal to the Crown. For Mexico, the coup challenged any semblance of legality and marked the beginning of violent and abrupt changes in government leadership that characterized much of nineteenth-century Mexican politics. Frank Tannenbaum writes in *Mexico: The Struggle for Peace and Bread* that the Peninsulares established a dangerous precedent because they "had broken the principle of the legal succession of power and had shown that the government could be overthrown in the middle of the night by a few armed men." . . .

Political Upheaval Continues into the 1820s

As the second decade of the nineteenth century came to an end, events in Spain again influenced the colony. Liberals had grown disenchanted with [restored King] Ferdinand's failure to abide by the 1812 constitution, which had been a stipulation of his restoration to the Spanish throne in 1814. In 1820, as the Crown enacted plans to send more troops to Mexico, liberal Spanish officers led by Rafael de Riego refused to follow the king's orders unless he accepted the 1812 constitution. With another threat to stability in Spain, questions again appeared concerning the direction of the colony and its relationship with Spain. In particular, conservatives feared the liberal policies being implemented in Spain. Among these were a more free press, an atmosphere conducive to frank and open discussion of policy, anticlerical policies, and the release of political prisoners who had participated in the insurgency movement in Mexico.

While conservatives grew nervous, royalist forces continued to pursue rebel leaders still operating in the countryside. Vicente Guerrero remained the primary target. Chasing after him was Augustin Iturbide, the royalist officer who had assisted in the arrest and execution of [José Maria] Morelos in 1815. Iturbide had managed to fall from grace with the viceroy due to his corrupt practices in the areas he controlled, but conservatives convinced the viceroy to place him at the head of the royal army so he could put down the rebel forces. In an impressive series of moves of deception and thievery, Iturbide acquired military control and the necessary funds to pursue Guerrero. But Iturbide learned he faced a daunting task in trying to capture the guerrilla leader, who had lived and fought for nearly a decade against the very soldiers trying to capture him. Rather than attempt to defeat him, Iturbide sought to have Guerrero join him. Following a series of negotiations and demonstrations of his real intentions, Iturbide convinced Guerrero to put down his arms and join in the movement declaring independence for Mexico.

In his position as head of the army, with the support of Guerrero, and together with other insurgents including Guadalaupe Victoria, Iturbide announced the Plan de Iguala on February 24, 1821. Iturbide's pronouncement initiated a precedent for political change that dominated Mexico until the twentieth century; all change followed pronunciation of a plan that outlined the change of government and the new direction being considered. Iturbide's plan consisted of three planks: (1) Mexico would declare independence from Spain, (2) Creoles and Peninsulares would receive equal treatment, and (3) the Catholic Church would remain the central form of religion (at the expense of religious intolerance for other religions). Another disturbing trend surfaced with Iturbide's plan—the role of the army in obtaining these goals. The army, which promised to uphold the Plan de Iguala, became known as the Army of the Three Guarantees. Creoles and Peninsulares now joined the flood of support for the Plan de Iguala. For the next six months the Spanish government, following the lead of the viceroy, attempted to stem the tide favoring independence, but the momentum was too great. Accompanied by the rebel leaders Vicente Guerrero and Guadalupe Victoria, Iturbide at the head of the Army of the Three Guarantees marched into Mexico City on September 27, 1821.

Mexico's independence came at a terribly high price. The political arena became a stage for great farce, scandal, assassination, deception, and thievery. In many ways it marked the condition of Mexico until the Reforma (the period from 1855 to 1876 during which the exponents of liberalism challenged the conservative traditions of the Church and military and sought to implement capitalism in Mexico) forced Mexico to examine its political and social organization and recognize the need for genuine change. Moreover, Iturbide's emergence as a political leader also marked the beginning of the era of the caudillo in Mexico's political arena. As elsewhere in Latin America, the country found itself repeatedly led by charismatic military leaders.

One can only speculate, but the independence achieved under the leadership of Iturbide would probably have surprised both Hidalgo and Morelos. It was a conservative movement more concerned about the preservation of elite status than the implementation of policies to advance equality to the masses. As a consequence, much of Hidalgo's social concerns were abandoned. The conservative social stratification, although gradually breaking down by the influence of capitalism in some areas, was still preserved, as people's status remained strongly influenced by race and skin color. In reality the nature of change in 1821 resulted in Mexico's independence from Spain, but at the cost of little variation in the quality of leadership. Very little changed, except that Creoles obtained what they had sought for centuries; replacement of Peninsulares in positions of leadership and influence.

EVENT 3 Liberia Is Founded as a Colony: January 1822

Liberia: American Blacks' Attempts at a Colony

by John H. Smyth

Liberia has an intriguing and troubled history. Established in North Africa by freed slaves who arrived in January 1822 with the help of the American Colonization Society, its state seal reads, "The love of liberty brought us here." Liberia was to be a place of opportunity, where people would be free of racism and violence and free to work for themselves, raise families, create communities, and govern themselves. Emigration from the United States, where the end of slavery was not yet in sight, was an attractive option to many blacks in the 1820s. Liberia continued to attract immigrants after the Civil War, when the status of blacks did not significantly improve.

In reality, however, the challenges faced by the new settlers were daunting. Initially, these challenges included land disputes, disease, and conflict with native tribes. Later, the challenges took political and economic forms as Liberia struggled for sovereignty, international recognition, and identity as neither Africans nor Americans.

In 1895, the second Congress on Africa met in Atlanta, Georgia, to provide a forum for discussion of African American issues such as emigration. John H. Smyth, who had served as minister to Liberia for nine years, delivered a speech about the meaning of Liberia to African Americans and about the more general importance of racial pride. He addressed misconceptions by whites and blacks, and challenged his fellow African Americans to make racially responsible choices.

John H. Smyth, *Lift Every Voice: African American Oratory, 1787–1900*, edited by Philip S. Foner and Robert James Branham. Tuscaloosa: University of Alabama Press, 1998. Copyright © 1998 by the University of Alabama Press. All rights reserved. Reproduced by permission.

In view of recent newspaper articles about migration of Negroes to Liberia, so much has been recently said by men of African descent of prominence, and by men of like prominence of uncertain descent, and by men of other races than the Negro, of Liberia and Africa generally, that I deem it a duty as an American citizen and a Negro, in vindication of the men and women of like descent with myself, citizens of the United States, to state some facts explanatory of and in rebuttal of much that has been said, ignorantly, unwisely and unsympathetically, to the detriment of the effort being made at self-government in Liberia, West Africa. The people who constitute the inhabitants and citizenship of Liberia (the largest portion of the latter class are American Negroes from the Southern part of the United States) are possessed of and imbued with the sentiment and the civilization peculiar to this section of our country. That these immigrant Negroes who migrated to West Africa, or began migration as far back as 1820, and who continue to go thither, have a better field there, with less embarrassing environment, to prove their capacity for self-government, for leadership in State-craft than their brethren in the northern, western and southern portions of the United States, will scarcely be seriously denied or questioned. This conceded, it seems to me that wisdom, self-respect, race loyalty, and American patriotism would show themselves richer to withhold judgment as to the success of the experiment being made in Africa for self-government until such time as this immigrant people and their descendants have lived in Liberia, Sierra Leone, the Gold Coast, the Camaroons and other parts of west Africa long enough to assimilate the sentiment of liberty and rule, the general heritage and possession of the native African, than it has shown itself in echoing the expression of opinion of white men, whatever their learning or literary capacity, who estimate the progress of the Negro by the standard of their own race with its superior opportunities, advantages and facilities.

Until we have demonstrated ability for organization, for government, and have shown effective cohesiveness and leadership here in the United States, it may be a little immodest to hastily and unadvisedly make up the record adverse to our immediate kith and kin, who less than sixty years ago made the first step on lines of independent form of government of themselves, and have successfully maintained themselves against the greed of Spain, the aggrandizement of France, and the envy and cupidity of the merchant class of England without active assistance or defense of our formidable North African squadron; without an army and without more than one gunboat, the property of the Republic.

Government and Economy of Young Liberia

Liberia is the only democratic republican form of government on the continent of Africa of which we have any knowledge. The civilization of the people constituting the majority of the citizenship of Liberia is American. It embraces that phase of our American system which has made the autonomy of the south distinct from that of all other parts of our common country. This is the resultant of the outgrowth of the laws and customs of the severalty as well as the jointness of that system of government which exists in the South. In so far as the civilization of the United States on analysis is differentiated as northern, southern, eastern, and western, and in the south as Virginian, Carolinian, Georgian, it may be said, that the people composing the nation have transferred such American phases of government to this part of Africa.

The pioneers of this colony, the descendants of them, and the immigrants that have gone from here at varying periods of time within sixty years, like those of us who have remained, have been the unhappy victims of the influences of an alien, racial oppression; are fragments of races and tribes, and lack much in capacity for maintaining a stable form of government without the aid which comes from the moral support of the United States. But notwithstanding the embarrassments and difficulties of this youthful nation, the elements of success are being gradually, surely and deeply laid in industrial and agricultural concerns. The masses of the people are directing their effort to agriculture, the development of the soil, and are leaving the matter of coast-commerce or barter to the few. . . .

Today's African American Is Displaced in Africa

We are taught by holy writ that God set bounds to the habitations of men. One race he established upon the continent of Africa, another upon the continent of Asia, another upon the continent of Europe, and a heterogeneity of races upon the continent of America, and fragmentary peoples inhabit the isles of the sea. In this various apportionment of races, wisdom and beneficence are shown. If we fail to see the former, we cannot doubt the latter, since "He does all things well."

In the light of these facts I fail to see a providence in bringing the Negro here, in making of him, at best, a moral and mental imitation of an original such as he can never be. Every step made by the Negro and his progeny, brought here a man and trained a slave, has continued him slave, though the institution as such has perished. The inherited taint of the institution has removed him further and further from the land of his fathers, from his tribal and racial traditions (valued heritages of a people), and has tended to make latent in him, if it has not wholly destroyed his best racial peculiarities and characteristics. In making us Anglo-Saxons by environment, we have lost not only in soul, but exteriorly, as objectified in the various types among us, nomenclatured colored people. However distasteful to the Caucasian the statement of the fact may be, the Negro who has grown to manhood under their alien Christian civilization, alien to the Negro and [in many respects] to Christ, is in his virtues and vices more Caucasian than African.

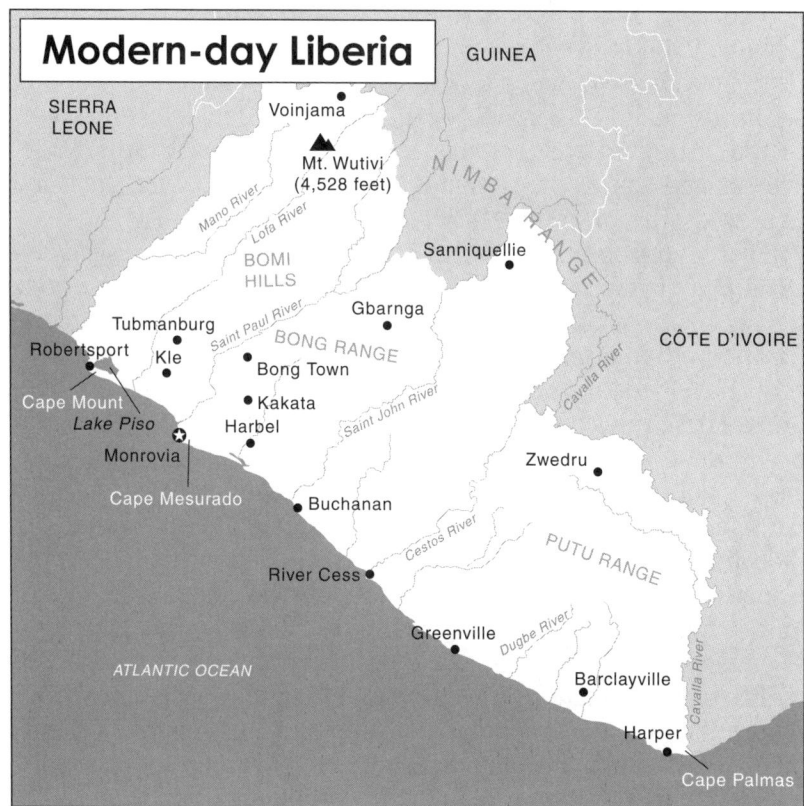

Africa's Rich Cultural and Historical Legacy Undermined

These considerations are serious to the Negro who feels any pride in being connected with races which aggregate, as known, more than 200,000,000 souls, who have an inalienable right to a continent as rich in its flora and fauna and mineral deposits (to say the least) as any other the sun warms with its heat and upon which the rains descend to make fruitful. Serious, indeed, must these considerations be to the Negro of the Americas and the Antilles, the descendants of those races whose moral elevation and mental ripeness in the morning of time manifested themselves in the conception and execution of those wonders of the ages, the pyramids, the sphynxes, and that musical colossus, Black Memnon, so fashioned that for two hundred years, on the rising of the god of day, as its rays shone upon it, it became musical with the concord of sweet sounds. Serious must these considerations be to the descendants of those races who erected these most beautiful temples and obelisks which have existed for centuries, the superscriptions within and upon which are yet to be interpreted by the descendants of Negro architects and builders; the ruins of which in their moral sublimity, stand as sentinels of time all along the delta and banks of the Nile, and are seen at Alexandria, Philae, Elephantine, Thebes and Karnac, representing their builders feeling after God in their desire for immortality.

These works of art and utility survive, in ruins, the perished civilizations of Asia, the cradle of the human race, and will survive the civilizations of Europe and this last, vigorous, Herculean civilization of America, which is but an evolution of Europe. These ruins have been the surprise and admiration of all other civilizations. These ruins have seen other civilizations in their dawn, their noontide, and will, notwithstanding the vandalism of the Caucasian, continue beyond his day. Those perished peoples of Africa furnished Europe with letters, sciences, and arts, although we, their lineal heirs, by the selfishness, greed, and ingratitude of the Caucasian, have been denied, until within the century, the title of human beings, and within three decades have only been regarded as equals before the law in a land of liberty and law. Two hundred and fifty years have removed us to a far greater distance from Africa than the geographical measurement that separates America from Africa, and to-day that continent is perhaps of less interest to the educated and refined Negro of America than to his thrifty, industrious, and adventurous white fellow-citizen.

There is error in a system of religion, a mistake in a system of education that so alienates brother from brother and sister from sister. Especially is this so when they trace their lineage from the same race stock. . . .

White Americans Do Not Understand African Americans

Though we are a part of this great national whole, we are a distinct and separate part, an alien part racially, and destined to be so by the immutable law of race pride, which is possessed by our white fellow-citizens, if not by us. The sentiment, the something stronger than sentiment which makes an English American proud of his connection with Britain, a French American proud of his connection with La Belle France, and a German American fondly attached to the memories of the fatherland, and all European races of their Aryan descent, has something that partakes of the moral sublime. Truly "language and religion do not make a race."

The characteristics, peculiarities, idiosyncrasies and habits have been determined by what has been displayed and noted of Negroes under influences foreign to them and beyond their control. This has been the cause of inaccurate knowledge of the races of Africa on the part of the whites, and inaccurate knowledge on the part of the Negroes themselves.

The elements of character of American whites are to be learned in the light of their free, unhampered ancestry and brethren in Europe.

African Americans Do Not Understand Themselves

The civilized Negro here has but recently emerged from slavery and been recognized a freeman; and though guaranteed in the possession of political rights, is still hampered by his inability to understand himself, by the conviction that on account of the political unity of the races here, his end must be reached by pursuit of the same line followed by the controlling races.

The condition of the race and present here makes the American Negro African, without the peculiarities of his race, an African only as to the hue of his skin and his blood. The black man here is Americanized, and as a sequence, sectionalized.

Now the difference between Africa in America, and Africa in

Africa being recognized, let us look to Africa in Africa. The races of Africa have not been a subject of Caucasian study.

Important Differences Among Africans Exist

The Egyptian, Carthaginian, and Moorish people are imperfectly known, and the interior, eastern, western races, are still more imperfectly understood, and for very prudential reasons,—the uncompromising conditions of climate toward European peoples, and the almost insuperable difficulties of ingress to the country. Says Amelia B. Edwards, in her cleverly written book, *A Thousand Miles up the Nile,* of African races:

> As with these fragments of the old tongue, so with the races, subdued again and again by invading hordes; intermixed for centuries together with Phoenician, Persian, Greek, Roman, and Arab blood, it fuses these heterogeneous elements in one common mould, reverts persistently to the early type, and remains African to the last. So strange is the tyranny of natural forces. The sun and soil of Africa demand one special breed of men, and will tolerate no other. Foreign residents cannot rear children in the country. In the Isthmus of Suez, which is considered the healthiest part of Egypt, an alien population of twenty thousand persons failed in the course of ten years to rear one infant born upon the soil. Children of an alien father and an Egyptian mother will die off in the same way in early infancy, unless brought up in simple native fashion. And it is affirmed of the descendants of mixed marriages, that after the third generation the foreign blood seems to be eliminated, while the traits of the race are restored in their original purity.

Another reason, race pride, so natural to all races, will always be a good and sufficient reason to deter the Saxon from recognizing excellences in a race foreign and alien to his race. Now, if we would know the Negro in his African home, we are to seek that knowledge of his true character through him.

The testimony of Africans, distinguished for their knowledge of their countrymen, for their learning and character, should be looked to, and consulted as authorities in these matters. The Arku and Ebo races are not to be known through the flippant and inconsiderate statements of some ignorant European who finds to his surprise and annoyance that he cannot successfully take advantage of them in a business transaction, and as a consequence declares the former people a deceptive, ignorant class, and the latter an insolent, lazy set. . . .

Liberia Needs Hard Workers, Not Idle Dreamers

It may not be inopportune or out of place to say, in the interest of the prospective immigrant and in the interest of Liberia, that it is perhaps unwise for persons to emigrate here simply for the purpose of being free and enjoying complete civil liberty and social equality. The State is young, and, though poor in developed resources, is vigorous in purpose and effort, and needy only of additional influences of civilization which are possessed by those who, at their homes, have displayed the ability of independent labor and proprietorship. That is to say, that the man needed as an immigrant here is one who, in his home, displays industry and fixedness of purpose sufficient to cause him to stick at work of some kind until he has earned and saved enough to purchase a comfortable home, is competent to control it and does control it, or a man who has entered upon a business and has self-denial enough to continue in it to the end of respectably supporting himself and family, or who has made himself a boost of some supporting trade—a man who is not directly dependent upon being a common servant, and who is not an ignorant laborer incapable of turning up something by his innate good sense and the God-given push within him.

Liberia possesses no large class of citizens who need or are able to employ a servant class from a foreign country. Intelligent laborers are needed, not ignorant ones. The constitution of this Republic guarantees to each immigrant so much cultivable land. The purpose of such grant is obvious; the improvement of it, the means of supporting one's self from the soil is the consideration for the gift, thereby winning from the forest and jungle valued lands capable of indefinite production, and winning from ignorance the native races by the pursuit of the arts of peace. Such results can be obtained alone through intelligent, persistent industry.

All agricultural labor, all coast labor, loading and unloading vessels, and fishing, all house service, are carried on, in general, by aborigines. Farm labor is worth from $2.50 to $4.00 per month, exclusive of housing and feeding. This is paid principally in goods, or one-half goods and the other half money. Where this labor is well fed, and treated well, it is honest and reliable—where these conditions are met there is no lack of it. The labor performed by the citizen class is farm proprietorship, trader, merchant, professional, and governmental. There is a minority of farm laborers of the civilized Liberian class.

Opportunity in Liberia Is Only Suited for Some

A clear understanding of the conditions of labor here is important to that class of foreign Negroes who contemplate settlement here. The possession of a few hundred dollars, skill in labor, and executive ability, constitute a capital that cannot but secure a most comfortable living here with a probability of wealth.

Unless the Negro out of Africa goes to Africa seeking a home because he has none; goes of his own volition, with as correct a knowledge of Africa as may be obtained from the writings of trustworthy African travelers and explorers and missionaries, reinforced by race loyalty, and with greater confidence in himself and his race than in any alien self and alien race; goes from a sense of duty imposed by his Christian enlightenment, and not unprovided with ability and previous experience to organize and control labor, with as ample means as he would go with from the Atlantic coast of the United States to the Pacific slope for the purpose of engaging in business, he is wholly and entirely unsuited for Africa, and would impede by his presence not only the progress of Liberia (if he went thither), but any part of Africa by his unprofitable presence, and ought to be denied the right to expatriate himself.

Racial Pride Should Grow Among African Americans

If by anything that I have said you have been impressed with the fact that you are descendants of African races and as a consequence that you are a separate and distinct people from Caucasian races, and that the highest excellence to which an individual can attain must be to work according to the bent of his genius, and the other to work in harmony with God's design in his creation, on his race line; if I have impressed you at all with the wisdom or propriety of confiding in the highest Negro authorities and the best alien writings; for reliable data respecting our race in the fatherland, and thereby awakened in you an interest and sincere desire for the well being of Africa and her races, for our people, and for accurate information concerning that most ancient, and most mysterious of lands; then I feel conscious of having made a contribution of information not wholly valueless to my countrymen that may tend to modify and dissipate general ignorance of us and of our antecedents and their country; and I have done something toward awakening your dormant self-respect, and given you some conception of the dignity which attaches to Negro manhood, and created in you a preference for your race before all other races; and this sentiment, if produced, will place you *en rapport* with the Negroes in Africa, who have no conception of any land greater, more beautiful than their own; any men braver and manlier than themselves, any women better, lovelier, and handsomer than African women. Then you will retire from this place with a feeling of stimulus rather than of satiety, of unrest rather than of repose; then shall I retire from my effort to interest you in Africa in Africa, and Africa in America with satisfied pride in having performed something of duty as a Negro—clear in his conviction of the high destiny in reserve for Africa and its races, and of your duty to be loyal to the race, since true allegiance will make us sharers in that glory which the sacred writing declares shall come, when Ethiopia shall stretch forth her hand unto God.

EVENT 4 The Monroe Doctrine: December 2, 1823

The Monroe Doctrine Establishes America's Political and Economic Independence from Europe

by Richard W. Leopold

The Monroe Doctrine represents a definitive statement of the political separation of the United States from Europe, and in particular from England. Although its effects were not immediate, it was a major foreign policy announcement. President James Monroe delivered his speech on December 2, 1823, and stated that America would no longer stand by while European powers interfered in areas of interest to the United States, both within and outside America's borders.

Because America's early history was closely connected with European politics, colonization, and related issues, even after independence, a definitive statement was needed to separate America from its European past. The Monroe Doctrine not only represented

---

Richard W. Leopold, *The Growth of American Foreign Policy: A History*. New York: Alfred A. Knopf, 1962.

America's commitment to its full independence and unique identity, but it put the force of the U.S. government behind that commitment.

Richard W. Leopold, professor of history at Northwestern University in Evanston, Illinois, reviews the legislative and circumstantial factors that led to the Monroe Doctrine in the following excerpt. He also explains the doctrine's political and military momentum in American history.

The Monroe Doctrine was the third major concept underlying American foreign policy before 1889. Although this principle was not precisely defined until December, 1823, or fully accepted until the Civil War, it too reflected the colonial desire to be spared the turmoil and wars of Europe. Like [the other two concepts,] isolationism and neutrality, its aim was to promote the safety and interests of the United States, but the method differed. Isolationism was a self-imposed ban upon permanent alliances and involvement in the diplomatic affairs of other continents; its realization depended solely on America's own efforts. Neutrality was also a voluntary curb on the activities of American citizens in war and peace, as well as a limitation on foreign belligerents; its enjoyment was contingent upon the tolerance of the large maritime nations and the strength of the young democratic government. The Monroe Doctrine sought to restrict in a specific geographic area the operations of the European monarchies; it could be upheld only insofar as the republic had the will and the power to do so. To drive Europe from the Western Hemisphere was, before 1889, an impossible task, but to confine and eventually nullify her influence was a legitimate and continuing goal. To limit, not eliminate, the activity of the Old World in the New was the cardinal objective of the Monroe Doctrine.

Historical Background of the Monroe Doctrine

Those passages in the message of December 2, 1823, that contain the Monroe Doctrine in its pristine form were a blend of past experience and current exigencies. From the colonial era came the theory of the two spheres, a belief—a fervent hope—that the diplomatic concerns of the two hemispheres could be kept apart. This idea can be traced to the Anglo-French Treaty of Whitehall in 1686, which provided that a war between colonies in the New World would not automatically lead to hostilities in the Old and, conversely, that a conflict in Europe should not, in itself, precipitate fighting in the Americas. This concept also paralleled isolationism; in his Farewell Address Washington wrote that "Europe has a set of primary interests which to us have none or a very remote relation." A quarter of a century later Secretary of State John Quincy Adams restated the theory when he told his minister in Russia on July 5, 1820, that "for the repose of Europe as well as of America, the European and American political systems should as separate and distinct from each other as possible." In advising Monroe how to handle Britain's proposal for an Anglo-American warning to the Continental monarchies to let alone the rebellious Spanish colonies, Jefferson declared on October 24, 1823: "America, North and South, has a set of interests distinct from those of Europe, and peculiarly her own."

A more immediate antecedent of the Monroe Doctrine was contemporary opposition to further European colonization in the New World. Although this hostility was implicit in the expansionist dreams of the young republic, it remained for John Quincy Adams to state it explicitly. While discussing a disputed boundary with the British minister on January 26, 1821, he exclaimed: "Keep what is yours, but leave the rest of the Continent to us." On July 17, 1823, he announced to the Russian envoy "that the American continents are no longer subjects for any new European colonial establishments." Five days later he instructed Richard Rush in London to emphasize the noncolonization principle in his forthcoming negotiations with Great Britain and Russia.

One way of reducing European influence in the Americas was to prevent the staking out of new claims. Another, though more indirect, was to bar the transfer of existing colonies from one nation to another. Strategically situated territory might be less dangerous to the republic if it belonged to a weak Spain rather than a powerful England. As early as January 25, 1786, Jefferson observed that the Gulf coast, which encompassed the mouths of many rivers that drained the interior, could not be in better hands for the time being; but he feared lest it be wrested from Spain before the United States was strong enough to do the acquiring itself. This apprehension, voiced privately, was repeated with variations in official dispatches at the turn of the century, when it seemed likely that Louisiana and both the Floridas would become part of a new French empire in North America. The United States resolutely opposed such a transfer, and alarm over its prospect prompted Jefferson to talk in 1802 of marrying the British fleet the day Napoleon took over New Orleans.

In 1811 this no-transfer policy finally received the sanction of both the executive and legislative branches. Worried lest England seize the Floridas, President Madison secretly asked Congress on January 3 to declare in executive session that such a move would jeopardize the nation's security. Twelve days later he signed a joint resolution which affirmed that the United States could not "without serious inquietude" see any part of the Floridas pass to a foreign power and that, under certain conditions, it might have to control the territory temporarily. The conditions were two: a request for protection by local Spanish officials and a threat of prior occupation by a European monarchy. In short, the United States was not content simply to express opposition to the transfer of colonies; it might even use force to prevent that transfer.

Florida was not the only Spanish dependency whose cession to a European nation was objected to in Washington. Writing to his minister in Madrid on April 28, 1823, Adams conceded that "the transfer of Cuba to Great Britain would be an event unpropitious to the interests of this Union." That understatement, however, was not followed by an appeal to Congress to authorize, even provisionally, an anticipatory occupation of the Pearl of the Antilles. Nor did the no-transfer principle find its way into the President's message of December 2, 1823. It continued, nonetheless, to be applied to other sites—such as Puerto Rico on October 25, 1825— and by 1870 it had come to be regarded as an essential part of the Monroe Doctrine.

Security Threats in 1823 Prompted Monroe to Act

Such were some of the precedents upon which James Monroe and his advisers could draw when they were confronted by a potential crisis in the summer and autumn of 1823. To a vague threat that Russia and Great Britain were about to enlarge their North American holdings was added the fear that the Quadruple Alliance, or a segment thereof, was planning to reconquer the recently recognized Latin American republics. In April, acting under a mandate from the Congress of Verona, French troops crossed the Pyrenees to restore the monarchy in Spain, and rumors were rife that those energies would soon be turned to establishing Bourbon princes on thrones in the New World. To the apprehensive, Cuba seemed menaced by both England and France. To devout republicans, the apparent crushing of the Greek bid for independence was another blow to the cause of liberty. Should not the United States grasp Canning's bid of August 16, 1823, and with England stem this surging tide of reaction? . . .

The Doctrine Separated American and European Authority

As stated in 1823, the Monroe Doctrine left untouched existing European dependencies in the New World but forbade future colonization. The transfer of monarchical institutions across the Atlantic was said to be dangerous to the safety of the United States, while any European interference in the domestic concerns of the Latin republics was branded as an unfriendly act. So long as Spain alone attempted reconquest, the United States would remain neutral; but that attitude might change if Madrid secured assistance from others. Finally, this country would abstain from participating in any war outside of the Western Hemisphere until its interests were directly affected or its rights menaced.

There were certain topics on which the Doctrine, as originally set forth, was silent. It did not define European interposition or interference in the New World. It said nothing about the adjustment of boundary disputes, the forcible collection of debts, the transfer of colonies from one European state to another, or the voluntary cession or territory by an American republic to a European monarchy. Monroe did not indicate that the United States might be more concerned with developments in the Caribbean than in Patagonia; in no place did he pledge the nation to use force to uphold the principles he enunciated. Nor did he give an unqualified promise never to take part in Europe's wars.

Almost at once men at home and abroad asked what Monroe meant and what he would do if the potential peril from the allied autocracies became actual. Since Congress alone could authorize military and naval measures, the views of the legislature were most significant. The failure of the President to seek them in advance and to make any recommendation for strengthening the armed forces suggests that he did not anticipate having to back up his words with deeds. Although most lawmakers appeared to endorse the warning to Europe, they were not eager to record that opinion officially. In fact, if it had not been for a pro-Hellenic bloc which resented Monroe's seeming indifference to the Greek cause and which sponsored demands to send an agent to Athens, Congress might never have discussed the Monroe Doctrine in the winter of 1823. But with the Hellenists forcing his hand, on January 20, 1824, Clay introduced a joint resolution avowing that the American people "would not see, without serious inquietude, any forcible interposition by the Allied Powers of Europe in behalf of Spain to reduce to their former subjection those parts of the continent" which had won their independence. The only real opposition in the House came from John Randolph of Virginia, a chronic dissenter and a bitter foe of Clay. Either because of the link to the Greek question or because it was learned that French intervention in the Western Hemisphere was unlikely, Clay's resolution was never brought to a vote in the House or even discussed in the Senate. Legislative inaction, however, did not signify disagreement. During the Panama debate two years later several speakers strongly supposed Monroe's position.

Interpretation and Application of the Doctrine

How did the Monroe administration and its successor, headed by Adams and Clay, interpret the Doctrine? Was it a maxim to be applied universally, or was it to be restricted to specific situations? Since the posture of the United States on the world scene hardly justified needless invocations, caution was the order of the day. Thus, by recognizing Brazil's independence on May 26, 1824, the government at Washington revealed that it would tolerate monarchies in the Americas if they represented the wishes of the people. To Colombia on August 6, 1824, Secretary Adams disclosed that he did not object to the employment of Spanish troops in the New World while France controlled the Iberian homeland. That same note evaded Colombia's bid for a defensive alliance against European interlopers and said that Congress must decide, after England had been consulted, how the United States would resist armed intervention from abroad. On December 7, 1824, Monroe told the legislature that the Latin American countries were free to adopt any institutions they desired. On April 13, 1825, Secretary of State Clay assured Brazil that its request for an alliance against Portugal was premature and that the United States would remain neutral in wars between a former colony and the mother country.

Lastly, on November 9, 1825, Clay ignored Mexico's plea for aid against an alleged French menace. In short, during the supposed crisis of 1823 President Monroe did not seek the cooperation, military or diplomatic, of the other American republics; in the calmer days of 1825 President Adams evinced no desire for a hemispheric system of reciprocal assistance. . . .

The Doctrine in the 1830s and 1840s

From 1826 to 1845 the Monroe Doctrine was not only virtually forgotten; it was also frequently violated. The noncolonization feature was the chief victim, and England was the main culprit. In one way or another Britain extended its sovereignty over the Falkland Islands in 1833, over Roatán in the Gulf of Honduras in 1838, and over San Juan del Norte in Nicaragua in 1841. England pushed the frontier of Belize steadily southward between 1833 and 1836, at the expense of the Central American Federation. But these transgressions were in remote regions, not vital to the security of the United States, and thus passed unchallenged even by President Jackson. The noninterference aspect of the Doctrine was not so badly breached. In 1838 France did institute a naval blockade of both Mexico and Argentina. In the first case, Mexican citizens were fired upon; in the second, French forces occupied an island in the River Plate and French officers meddled in Argentina's domestic affairs. But these reprisals, like others undertaken by England, were designed to secure unpaid claims, not subvert existing regimes. They did elicit from Congress a request for information, but that body did not yet consider that collecting debts by force fell under Monroe's interdict.

When European activity occurred closer to home, the United States manifested more concern. By the early 1840's the expansionist impulse to annex Texas and California and to settle the Oregon dispute was growing rapidly, yet in each of those areas England or France or both seemed to be trying to thwart American ambitions. In Oregon, open on terms of equality to citizens of both nations under the treaty of 1827, the Hudson's Bay Company was attempting to divert the influx of pioneers. In Texas, Anglo-French representatives were striving to patch up a peace between that republic and Mexico; and they were prepared to guarantee Texan independence by a diplomatic act, in which the United States could join or not as it saw fit. In California, loosely governed from Mexico City, there was talk of a European protectorate and even of outright cession. These schemes, which never got far beyond the blueprint stage, were based on the assumption, blatantly expressed in June, 1845, by Prime Minister Francois Guizot, that Europe must maintain a balance of power in North America to curb the westward march of the young republic. Although this idea of a balance of power did negate the theory of the two spheres, there was nothing in the original Doctrine to prohibit independent Mexico from ceding California to France. Nor could the Doctrine be invoked to require the Oregon boundary to be drawn at a particular place.

Nevertheless, if an appeal to Monroe's memory bolstered his diplomacy as trouble loomed over Texas, Oregon, and California, James K. Polk was not one to hold back. With virtually no foreshadowing, with very little discussion in the cabinet, and with only an occasional talk with a congressional leader, the President revived and reoriented the principles which had lain dormant for two decades. In his message of December 2, 1845, he began, as Monroe had begun twenty-two years before, with foreign affairs. He branded Anglo-French action in Texas as "interference" and prophesied that similar "intrigues" elsewhere would also fall. He did not, however, speak directly of California. After a long review of the Mexican and Oregon problems, Polk turned to the balance-of-power theory and denied that it could apply to the Western Hemisphere. Europe must keep its hands off the New World, just as the United States abstained from involvement in the Old. The American people would resist any attempt by foreign powers, in the name of the balance of power, to restrict their expansion. . . .

The Doctrine in the 1850s and 1860s

The 1850's saw added publicity given to the message of 1823. During a debate in January, 1853, Monroe's pronouncement was for the first time consistently referred to in Congress and in the press as a "doctrine." Theretofore such words as "principle" and "declaration" had been employed. On January 6, 1854, the Doctrine was appealed to for the first time in a diplomatic note to another country. In June, 1856, the Democratic platform began the now familiar practice of lauding the Doctrine. Yet this evidence should not obscure the fact that prior to 1861 the Monroe Doctrine was still not accepted by all citizens as a sound and incontrovertible policy, to be invoked whenever their interests in the Western Hemisphere seemed menaced. It had never been formally endorsed by Congress. To many it looked like the property of expansionist-minded Democrat, and those of cautious temperament preferred not to act in its name until the need was clearly apparent and unless the people were prepared to back words with deeds.

What transformed the Monroe Doctrine from a diplomatic principle of limited utility with distinct partisan overtones into a dogma of universal application, concurred in by all Americans irrespective of political ties, was the challenge it encountered between 1861 and 1867. Before that period it had been challenged and even violated, but rarely in areas so vital to the national security and never with so flagrant a disregard of public opinion. Earlier infringements—such as the seizure of the distant Falklands, the extension of the Belize frontier through the Central American jungle, the occupation of tiny Roatán in the Gulf of Honduras—and previous threats in Texas and California pale into insignificance before the reannexation of the Dominican Republic by Spain in 1861 and the re-establishment of a monarchy in Mexico by France in 1864.

For present purposes, the details of those challenges are less important than the reaction they aroused in the United States. At the diplomatic level the response had to be restrained. Not until April, 1865, when the Union was restored and its huge armed forces were free to be turned against foreign interlopers, could [Secretary of State William H.] Seward back words with deeds. By then the restoration of Spanish rule in Haiti had collapsed; by then trouble in Europe and resistance in Mexico prompted Napoleon III to think of liquidating the ill-starred venture; by then, after early mistakes, Seward was moving with consummate skill. Never invoking the words of the fifth President but always speaking his language, the Secretary made it clear that sooner or later the twin principles of noncolonization and noninterference in the New World would be vindicated, by might if need be. At the popular level there was less restraint. Inveighing against France or Spain and cheering for the Monroe Doctrine were useful ways of releasing frustrated emotions during the dreary months before the tide turned in favor of the North. Beginning in 1862, giant rallies pledged allegiance to the principles of 1823. Famous men of the day spoke out in their behalf; writings more hortatory than historical poured from the press. Even an organization named the Defenders of the Monroe Doctrine was formed.

Public agitation precipitated congressional action. Against the known wishes of Lincoln and Seward, resolutions were introduced condemning France and requesting the administration to compel withdrawal from Mexico. Thanks to Sumner, all such moves in the Senate were buried in the Foreign Relations Committee, but by 1864 delay was no longer possible in the House. Without a dissenting vote that chamber on April 4 resolved that "it does not accord with the policy of the United States to acknowledge any monarchical government erected on the ruins of any republican government in America under the auspices of any European Power." Although it mentioned no names, the House had in mind French interference in Mexico's internal strife and the transfer of monarchical institutions from the Old World to the New. At the cost of an unpleasant controversy with the chairman of the Foreign Affairs Committee involving recognition rather than the Monroe Doctrine, the executive managed to retain control of Mexican affairs and by steady but dignified pressure contributed to the evacuation of Napoleon's troops in 1867.

The Doctrine in the 1870s and 1880s

From 1867 to 1889 the Monroe Doctrine continued to grow quietly. Two trends may be noted. One was the final consolidation of the no-transfer principle with the Doctrine itself. This was effected in President Ulysses Grant's message to Congress on May 31, 1870, and in Secretary Hamilton Fish's memorandum to the Senate on July 14, 1870, although as late as August, 1877, there was no protest from Washington when the government of Norway and Sweden sold the Caribbean island of St. Bartholomew to France. The second was a contention that the construction of an interoceanic canal in the Western Hemisphere by a European state violated the Monroe Doctrine. On June 25, 1879, Ambrose E. Burnside, Republican of Rhode Island and better remembered for his military than his senatorial career, offered a resolution terming a foreign-built canal dangerous to the nation's peace and safety; and he rested his case on the message of 1823. On May 8, 1882, Secretary of State Frederick T. Frelinghuysen invoked the Doctrine in an attempt to persuade Great Britain to abrogate the Clayton-Bulwer Treaty [a compromise to ease competition between Britain and the U.S. in Central America]. Although the Burnside resolution failed to pass and the English refused to heed Frelinghuysen's plea, these new pretensions foreshadowed a further growth that occurred at the turn of the century.

By the time the French withdrew from Mexico, the Monroe Doctrine had come of age. Promulgated but qualified in the 1820's, forgotten and violated in the 1830's, revived but disputed in the 1840's, publicized but monopolized by one party in the 1850's, it had emerged from the ordeal of the 1860's strengthened and acclaimed, enshrined as never before in the hearts of the American people. With new pretensions advanced in its name after 1867, no responsible statesmen on either side of the Atlantic dared—though a few might try—to ignore the powerful prejudice in the United States against any type of intervention by the Old World in the affairs of the New.

EVENT 4

The Monroe Doctrine: December 2, 1823

The United States Opposes European Intervention in the Western Hemisphere

by James Monroe

On December 2, 1823, President James Monroe delivered a speech to Congress detailing what would come to be known as the Monroe Doctrine. Monroe was concerned about Russia's intention to ban all but Russian ships from a certain length of America's northwest coastline. Additionally, European powers were rumored to be planning to recapture Spanish American republics that had gained independence from Spain. These concerns led the president to wonder if European powers might consider the reconquest of the United States.

In light of these perceived threats and international meddling by European nations, Monroe determined that the time had come for the United States to assert itself as a truly sovereign nation. According to Monroe, no longer would European nations be allowed to intervene in U.S. domestic affairs, including its land and coastlines. This was an important step in America's maturity as an independent

James Monroe, address to the U.S. Congress, Washington, DC, December 2, 1823.

nation intent on keeping and protecting its people and territory.

James Monroe was the fifth president of the United States and a major figure in the establishment of Thomas Jefferson's Republican Party. Monroe fought heroically in the American Revolution. After the war he practiced law and began a political career that included offices as congressman, senator, minister to France, governor of Virginia, secretary of state, and finally president (1817–1825).

At The Proposal of the Russian Imperial Government, made through the minister of the Emperor residing here, a full power and instructions have been transmitted to the minister of the United States at St. Petersburg, to arrange, by amicable negotiation, the respective right and interests of the two nations on the northwest coast of this continent. A similar proposal has been made by his Imperial Majesty to the Government of Great Britain, which has likewise been acceded to. The Government of the United States has been desirous, by the friendly proceeding, of manifesting the great value which they have invariably attached to the friendship of the Emperor, and their solicitude to cultivate the best understanding with his Government. In the discussions to which this interest has given rise, and in the arrangements by which they may terminate, the occasion has been judged proper for asserting as a principle in which the rights and interests of the United States are involved, that the American continents, by the free and independent condition which they have assumed and maintain, are henceforth not to be considered as subjects for future colonization by any European powers.

It was stated at the commencement of the last session that a great effort was then making in Spain and Portugal to improve the condition of the people of those countries, and that it appeared to be conducted with extraordinary moderation. It need scarcely be remarked that the result has been, so far, very different from what was then anticipated. Of events in that quarter of the globe with which we have so much intercourse, and from which we derive our origin, we have always been anxious and interested spectators. The citizens of the United States cherish sentiments the most friendly in favor of the liberty and happiness of their fellow-men on that side of the Atlantic. In the wars of the European powers in matters relating to themselves we have never taken any part, nor does it comport with our policy so to do. It is only when our rights are invaded or seriously menaced that we resent injuries or make preparation for our defense. With the movements in this hemisphere we are, of necessity, more immediately connected, and by causes which must be obvious to all enlightened and impartial observers. The political system of the allied powers is essentially different in this respect from that of America. This difference proceeds from that which exists in their respective Governments. And to the defense of our own, which has been achieved by the loss of so much blood and treasure, and matured by the wisdom of the their most enlightened citizens, and under which we have enjoyed unexampled felicity, this whole nation is devoted. We owe it, therefore, to candor, and to the amicable relations existing between the United Sates and those powers, to declare that we should consider any attempt on their part to extend their system to any portion of this hemisphere as dangerous to our peace and safety. With the existing colonies or dependencies of any European power we have not interfered and shall not interfere. But with the governments who have declared their independence and maintained it, and whose independence we have, on great consideration and on just principles, acknowledged, we could not view any interposition for the purpose of oppressing them, or controlling in any other manner their destiny, by any European power, in any other light than as the manifestation of an unfriendly disposition toward the United States. In the war between these new governments and Spain we declared our neutrality at the time of their recognition, and to this we have adhered and shall continue to adhere, provided no change shall occur which, in the judgment of the competent authorities of this Government, shall make a corresponding change on the part of the United States indispensable to their security.

James Monroe

The late events in Spain and Portugal show that Europe is still unsettled. Of this important fact no stronger proof can be adduced than that the allied powers should have thought it proper, on any principle satisfactory to themselves, to have interposed by force, in the internal concerns of Spain. To what extent such interposition may be carried, on the same principle, is a question in which all independent powers whose governments differ from theirs are interested, even those most remote, and surely none more so than the United States. Our policy in regard to Europe, which was adopted at an early stage of the wars which have so long agitated that quarter of the globe, nevertheless remains the same, which is, not to interfere in the internal concerns of government for us; to cultivate friendly relations with it, and to any of its powers; to consider the government de facto as the legitimate preserve those relations by a flank, firm, and manly policy, meeting, in all instances, the just claims of every power, submitting to injuries from none. But in regard to these continents, circumstances are eminently and conspicuously different. It is impossible that the allied powers should extend their political system to any portion of either continent without endangering our peace and happiness; nor can anyone believe that our southern brethren, if left to themselves, would adopt it of their own accord. It is equally impossible, therefore, that we should behold such interposition, in any form, with indifference. If we look to the comparative strength and resources of Spain and those new governments, and their distance from each other, it must be obvious that she can never subdue them. It is still the true policy of the United States to leave the parties to themselves, in the hope that other powers will pursue the same course.

Particular Emphasis on Relationship with England

The Monroe doctrine finds its recognition in those principles of international law which are based upon the theory that every nation shall have its rights protected and its just claims enforced.

Of course this Government is entirely confident that under the sanction of this doctrine we have clear rights and undoubted claims. Nor is this ignored in the British reply. The prime minister, while not admitting that the Monroe doctrine is applicable to present conditions, states: "In declaring that the United States would resist any such enterprise if it was contemplated, President Monroe adopted a policy which received the entire sympathy of the English Government of that date." He further declares: "Though the language of President Monroe is directed to the attainment of objects which most Englishmen would agree to be salutary, it is impossible to admit that they have been inscribed by any adequate authority in the code of international law." Again he says: "They (Her Majesty's Government) fully concur with the view which President Monroe apparently entertained, that any disturbance of the existing territorial distribution in the hemisphere by any fresh acquisitions on the part of any European state, would be a highly inexpedient change."

In the belief that the doctrine for which we contend was clear and definite, that it was founded upon substantial considerations and involved our safety and welfare, that it was fully applicable to our present conditions and to the state of the world's progress and that it was directly related to the pending controversy and without any conviction as to the final merits of the dispute, but anxious to learn in a satisfactory and conclusive manner whether Great Britain sought, under a claim of boundary, to extend her possessions on this continent without right, or whether she merely sought possession of territory fairly included within her lines of ownership, this Government proposed to the Government of Great Britain a resort to arbitration as the proper means of settling the question to the end that a vexatious boundary dispute between the two contestants might be determined and our exact standing and relation in respect to the controversy might be made clear.

Despite Tension, United States Will Hold Firm to Doctrine

It will be seen from the correspondence herewith submitted that this proposition has been declined by the British Government, upon grounds which in the circumstances seem to me to be far from satisfactory. It is deeply disappointing that such an appeal actuated by the most friendly feelings towards both nations directly concerned, addressed to the sense of justice and to the magnanimity of one of the great powers of the world and touching its relations to one comparatively weak and small, should have produced no better results.

The course to be pursued by this Government in view of the present condition does not appear to admit of serious doubt. Having labored faithfully for many years to induce Great Britain to submit this dispute to impartial arbitration, and having been now finally apprised of her refusal to do so, nothing remains but to accept the situation, to recognize its plain requirements and deal with it accordingly. Great Britain's present proposition has never thus far been regarded as admissible by Venezuela, though any adjustment of the boundary which that country may deem for her advantage and may enter into of her own free will can not of course be objected by the United States.

Assuming, however, that the attitude of Venezuela will remain unchanged, the dispute has reached such a stage as to make it now incumbent upon the United States to take measures to determine with sufficient certainty for its justification what is the true divisional line between the Republic of Venezuela and British Guiana. The inquiry to that end should of course be conducted carefully and judicially and due weight should be given to all available evidence records and facts in support of the claims of both parties.

Appeal to Congress for Support

In order that such an examination should be prosecuted in a thorough and satisfactory manner I suggest that the Congress make an adequate appropriation for the expenses of a commission, to be appointed by the Executive, who shall make the necessary investigation and report upon the matter with the least possible delay. When such report is made and accepted it will in my opinion be the duty of the United States to resist by every means in its power as a willful aggression upon its rights and interests the appropriation by Great Britain of any lands or the exercise of governmental jurisdiction over any territory which after investigation we have determined of right belongs to Venezuela.

In making these recommendations I am fully alive to the responsibility incurred, and keenly realize all the consequences that may follow.

I am nevertheless firm in my conviction that while it is a grievous thing to contemplate the two great English-speaking peoples of the world as being otherwise than friendly competitors in the onward march of civilization, and strenuous and worthy rivals in all the arts of peace, there is no calamity which a great nation can invite which equals that which follows a supine submission to wrong and injustice and the consequent loss of national self-respect and honor beneath which are shielded and defended a people's safety and greatness.

EVENT 5: The Decembrist Uprising: December 14, 1825

The Decembrist Revolt Signals the Start of Russia's Revolutionary History

by Anatole G. Mazour

Russian history records numerous revolts and uprisings as the Russian people attempted to topple repressive regimes or press for reforms. Tracing the roots of this revolutionary history ultimately leads to a failed revolt on December 14, 1825. This uprising, known as the Decembrist revolt, was unique in that it sought not only to overthrow the existing regime, but also to replace it with a new one. It was the first glimpse of the chasm that existed between Russia's liberal, action-oriented thinkers and the traditional government systems.

In the early nineteenth century, peacetime conditions, the Russian people suffered from poverty and other hardships. Many were embittered when czar Peter the Great's affection for modern Western ideas and practices failed to signal improvements in their daily lives. When reform did not materialize, groups of aristocratic young men created secret societies to discuss how to bring about change in their government. These groups soon turned revolutionary in nature. They wanted to overthrow Peter's successor, Alexander I, and in-

---

Anatole G. Mazour, *Russia: Past and Present*. New York: Van Nostrand, 1951.

stall a dictatorship that would pave the way for a more republican form of government in Russia.

When the childless Alexander died in 1825 and the line of succession was temporarily uncertain, the revolutionaries saw their chance to act. On December 14, the Decembrists made their move. Unfortunately for them, they overestimated their support and lacked a strong plan for actually seizing power from the likely czar, Alexander's brother Nicholas. Nicholas answered the revolt of three thousand with fifteen thousand imperial troops. The revolutionaries were decimated, and those who survived faced extremely harsh punishment. At first the five most culpable were sentenced to be drawn and quartered, and the rest to be hanged. Nicholas, however, commuted the sentences to hangings for the five and exile for the rest.

Anatole G. Mazour, the author of the following overview of the Decembrist revolt, taught history at Stanford University. He is the author of four books about Russian political history.

The Decembrist uprising of 1825 . . . registers in history an important step in the revolutionary development of Russia. Prior to 1825 most of the uprisings carried a strong indigenous imprint, whereas the Decembrist revolt was the first consequence of Russia's full entrance into Western European political and military life. Western influence upon Russian society had been felt ever since the reign of Peter, but not until 1825 did it express itself in the form of an underground political movement with the ultimate intention of social reform along Western revolutionary lines. The French Revolution began to determine the political and social climate as far as the banks of the Neva. It is not within the scope of this chapter to trace the roots of Decembrism except to point out the basic revolutionary sources. Rivulets of political philosophy had been slowly running eastward since the end of the eighteenth century. Through foreign tutors in Russia and Russian students and travelers in Western Europe, current political teachings were penetrating the cultural isolationism of the country. Then came the Napoleonic Wars, the invasion of Moscow and the reverberating effects—the Russian army in the heart of Europe. Thousands upon thousands of soldiers and young officers, after visiting the Western countries, could no longer accept the existing conditions at home. Witnessing the complete collapse of the old order abroad they could no more accept it in Russia than the French bourgeois had accepted it in France. Through personal contacts, through the joining of Masonic orders, through attendance at universities and participation in various circles, the young men of Russia carried with them eastward the revolutionary seed to be planted in alien soil.

Social and Philosophical Foundations

It is obvious that the process of cultivation of Western ideas in Russia was not a task for the peasant masses, although it was intended for their benefit. It was almost exclusively a task of the educated classes, which in reality meant the aristocracy. The revolutionary phase, therefore, into which Russia entered at this time, was largely carried out by an aristocratic element whose members were inspired by liberal idealism and guided by humanitarian principles. It was not a mass movement such as that of Pugachev [a rebel leader whose efforts were crushed in 1773]; on the contrary, the new leaders feared the masses. They were an active minority hoping to accomplish reform for the sake of the majority. The political opposition this time had more clearly defined aims than the mass uprisings of the previous centuries: instead of such vague slogans as lower taxes, freedom from military service, or land and freedom for the peasants, politically minded men now insisted upon "constitutional rights" or "guarantees of liberties," complete or partial nationalization of the land, limited powers of the monarch or a republican form of government, a federal system or highly centralized national authority. In short, an intellectual quality was now added to the revolutionary movement.

Importance of Secret Societies

How was the designated political program to be achieved? By persuasion or by force? Opinions varied. The prevailing view was that persuasion was desirable, although if force became necessary it should be used; some, however, believed in outright regicide. Meanwhile, to be prepared for any emergency, it was believed that an effective secret organization must be maintained. This was definitely an imported idea, for ever since the French Revolution and particularly since the fall of Napoleon, Western Europe had been engaged in a battle against reaction. The secret Masonic lodges, the German Tugendbund, the Greek Haeteria, and the Italian Carbonari all served as models for the early Russian conspirators. The first secret society was organized about 1816–17, under the name of The Union of Salvation, later renamed the Welfare Society; this in turn gave rise to the so-called Northern and Southern Societies, one operating in the capital, the other in the Ukraine. The latter also established cooperation with another society known as the United Slavs. Most of these secret organizations were made up of military men, chiefly of the aristocratic classes, participants in the campaigns against France.

If one is to characterize the ideological physiognomy of these secret societies, it must be said first that practically all their members were fired with extreme patriotism and nationalism. Partly, after having witnessed Western European progress, they suffered a sense of shame for their fatherland's backwardness; partly they represented the pioneers of the later social type in Russia—the repenting nobleman who was moved by a deep sense of social and humanitarian duty to strive for improved conditions for the masses. Whatever their political views and disagreements, they all agreed upon one thing—serfdom must be stamped out; and, through the creation of favorable conditions for trade and commerce, the rising Russian bourgeoise must be allowed a more respectable place in society. Such a program could be attained, most of them believed, through the establishment of a representative system of government, and through administrative and judicial reforms. Some leading participants even drafted constitutional charters for the future "Young Russia." While one of them, Muraviev, was influenced by the federal system of the United States, Pestel, that "socialist before socialism," insisted upon a highly centralized republican form of government.

The political and moral force of the Decembrists lies chiefly in their method of attaining their aims, in the faith of secret organizations, and in the martyrdom of their leaders. It can safely be stated that the entire nineteenth century revolutionary movement stems from the Decembrist revolt of 1825, when a handful of leaders endeavored to use the brief interregnum for their own end—to compel the new Emperor to adopt a constitution. It was perhaps all Quixotic, but what pioneering enterprise is entirely "practical"? Five of the leaders were hanged; hundreds received other sentences varying from Siberian exile for life to military service in the Caucasus. It was the first revolt that was carried from the confines of the Court to the broad Senate Square of St. Petersburg. The brave though "mad" venture inspired many a young man, in reverence to the Decembrist martyrs, to continue the fight against injustice. Among these were the outstanding members of the generation of the "forties."

The Decembrist Legacy

The December uprising left the Russian government in a trembling state, fearing any social disturbance at home or abroad. The chief prosecutor and gendarme of Russia was Nicholas I, who combined all the qualities for this task. The death of his father, preceding his brother's accession to the throne, and the five hangings coming just before his own coronation added little humor to his political outlook. And if on the whole he succeeded in muzzling the nation, he was less successful in aiding Metternich, his political God-father in Western Europe. Periodic convulsions on the Continent or in Poland, at the very doorstep of Russia, caused him fearful anxiety. Small wonder that whenever there appeared the remotest semblance of "sedition" the administration considered it the sign of the "Western plague" attacking the healthy national body.

Nevertheless, despite all precautions and police measures, the reign of Nicholas I (1826–1855) is not characterized by internal peace and harmony. The three decades register a goodly number of local disturbances, 674 peasant uprisings of various degrees, increasing as the years went by: between 1826–1834 there were 145 rebellions, whereas between 1845–1854 there were no less than 348. Between 1834–1854 there are registered 250 assaults on landlords of which 173 resulted in murder. During the reign of Nicholas the army was called to suppress peasant uprisings in 228 estates and on 34 occasions the expeditions had to enter into regular battles. According to Professor Paul N. Miliukov's statistics the total number of serious rebellions, not including minor unrest, was 547; between 1835–1854, according to the same source, 144 landlords or their stewards were murdered and 75 assaults were registered with intention to murder. A more detailed list of uprisings, according to year, is given as follows:

1828	17	1843	19
1829	13	1844	34
1830	13	1845	31
1831	9	1846	16
1832	10	1847	31
1833	11	1848	64

1834	20	1849	25
1838	15	1850	21
1839	14	1851	28
1840	15	1852	44
1841	17	1853	33
1842	21	1854	23[1]

These uprisings were sporadic, mostly poorly organized and leaderless, usually ending with a punitive expedition, corporal punishment of participants, and exile of the instigators. Between 1835 and 1843 no less than 416 peasants were banished to Siberia.

From these figures we can state conclusively that, despite all the severe and vigilant police measures, the government did not succeed in whipping the peasantry into submission. The number of uprisings or assaults indicates that the peasants had no intention of accepting their lot without resistance.

---

[1]. Thomas G. Masaryk in his *Spirit of Russia* gives the following figures: (vol. I, pp. 130–31).

1826–30	41 Jacqueries	1840–44	101
1831–34	46 — —	1845–49	172
1835–39	59 — —	1850–59	137
		TOTAL	556

Mr. Masaryk adds: "Without exaggeration, 200 could certainly be added to this total. During the years 1855–1859, 152 landowners (among them 21 officials) were murdered, whilst there were 175 attempted murders."

EVENT 6

The Nat Turner Uprising: August 21–22, 1831

Panic After the Nat Turner Uprising Begins to Change Racial Attitudes Toward Slavery

by Herbert Aptheker

Nat Turner's 1831 slave revolt is considered the most significant such uprising in American history. It claimed more lives than other slave revolts, and it terrorized southerners, who came to see their slaves not as mindless laborers, but as potentially violent killers. Until then owners had a largely complacent attitude toward the institution of slavery and their control of the slave majority. Nat Turner's uprising shook their confidence in their ability to maintain that power. Debate over slavery took on new dimensions as people questioned the wisdom of such a system and how much longer it could continue as it had in the past. Some historians cite these debates as among the first important steps in the long road to abolition.

Turner's uprising was motivated not by the desire to liberate the slaves, but by his own sense of religious purpose. A lay preacher, Turner assured his followers that God had directed him to lead them against their oppressors. The revolt was carefully planned. On August 21 Turner led eight men to murder five members of the Travis family of Southampton County, Virginia. Over the next thirty-six

---

Herbert Aptheker, *American Negro Slave Revolts*. New York: Columbia University Press, 1943. Copyright © 1943 by Columbia University Press. All rights reserved. Reproduced by permission.

hours, Turner's band of slaves grew to some seventy men, and fifty-seven whites were killed before a group of armed locals put down the rebellion.

Turner himself fled into hiding, where he remained for six weeks before being captured on October 30. He faced serious charges: The dead included eighteen women and twenty-four children. Unrepentant, Turner accepted his judgment of execution and was hanged twelve days after his capture. However, his death did not allay the fears of the slave owners, whose sense of security and authority was permanently weakened.

Before his death in 2003, Herbert Aptheker was a leading scholar of black history and a lifelong political radical. He is the author of *Documentary History of the Negro People.*

Southampton is a tidewater county, located in the southeastern part of Virginia, bordering the state of North Carolina. Covering six hundred square miles, it was an important economic unit in the tidewater area. In 1830 it was second in the State in its production of potatoes and rice, and, in 1840, was the leading county in cotton production, in the value of its orchard produce, and in the number of its swine. Its population trend was that of the section, i.e., a more rapid growth of the Negro than of the white element. Thus, one finds that while, in 1820, there were 6127 whites and 8043 Negroes in Southampton County, in 1830 the figures read 6574 whites and 9501 Negroes. In 1830 out of a total of thirty-nine tidewater counties only three surpassed Southampton in the number of free Negroes, and only four in the number of slaves, and in the number of whites.

In its economic decline Southampton is also typical of the condition in eastern Virginia during the period. Thus, for example, it ranked fifth in the State in 1810 in the amount of taxes it paid on the assessed valuation of its land and lots, but dropped to forty-fourth in 1820 and to forty-sixth in 1830.

The situation, then, in the decade prior to the Southampton revolt is one of extraordinary *malaise* in the slaveholding area. It is marked by a considerable expansion and development of anti-slavery feeling, nationally and internationally (as part of an all-embracing upsurge of progressive and radical thought and action throughout the western world), by great and serious unrest among the slave populations, in the West Indies as well as on the Continent, by severe economic depression, and by the more rapid growth of the Negro population than the white throughout the old South. Testifying to the uneasiness of the master class there appear numerous precautionary measures for the purpose of overawing, or further restricting the activities of the slave population (which, in turn, very likely stimulated discontent), and, as a last resort, in order to assure the speedy suppression of all evidences of slave insubordination.

It was into such a situation (one is tempted to assert, though proof is, of course, not at hand, that it was *because* of such a situation) that the upraised dark arms of vengeance of Turner and his followers crashed in the summer of 1831.

Turner's Background and Personality

Nat Turner was born October 2, 1800, and apparently lived all his life in Southampton County. At the time of the rebellion he was:

> 5 feet 6 or 8 inches high, weighs between 150 and 160 pounds, rather bright complexion, but not a mulatto, broad shoulders, large flat nose, large eyes, broad flat feet, rather knockkneed, walks brisk and active, hair on the top of the head very thin, no beard, except on the upper lip and the top of the chin, a scar on one of his temples, also one on the back of his neck, a large knot on one of the bones of his right arm, near the wrist, produced by a blow.

Very naturally, William Lloyd Garrison, in commenting upon this description, pointed to these scars as important explanations for Turner's actions. But the Richmond *Enquirer* assured its readers that Turner got two of his bruises in fights with fellow slaves and one of them, that on his temple, through a mule's kick. [W.S.] Drewry [author of *The Southampton Insurrection*], notwithstanding the fact that his description of Turner hardly indicates a pugnacious individual, accepts the explanation of the southern newspaper, and points out, correctly, that Turner himself stated that his last master, Joseph Travis, had not been severe. But he had had other masters—Benjamin Turner and Putnam Moore—and he had, in 1826 or 1827, run away from one of these after a change in overseers.

However that may be, mere personal vengeance was not Nat Turner's motive. He had learned how to read—precisely when he did not know—and, when his labors permitted, he had immersed himself in the stories of the Bible. He was a keen, mechanically gifted man whose religion offered him a rationalization for his opposition to the status quo. Later writers have described him as an overseer or foreman, and while no convincing support for this has been found, it is certain that his considerable mental abilities were recognized and appreciated by his contemporaries. He was a religious leader, often conducting services of a Baptist nature and exhorting his fellow workers. It appears that even white people were influenced, if not controlled, by him, so that, as he said, he immersed one Ethelred T. Brantley and prevailed upon him to "cease from his wickedness."

Turner became convinced that he "was ordained for some great purpose in the hands of the Almighty." In the spring of 1828, while working in the fields, he "heard a loud noise in the heavens, and the Spirit instantly appeared to me and said the Serpent was loosened, and Christ had laid down the yoke he had borne for the sins of men, and that I should take it on and fight against the Serpent, for the time was fast approaching when the first should be last and the last should be first."

"Signs" Compel Turner to Plan Revolt

The slave waited for a sign from his God. This came to him in the form of the solar eclipse of February 12, 1831. Then apparently for the first time, he told four other slaves of his plans for rebellion. All joined him, and these American Negroes selected the Fourth of July as the day on which to strike for liberty, a choice which led a later commentator to curse them because they had "perverted that sacred day."

Turner was ill on the "sacred day," and the conspirators waited for another sign. This appeared to them on Saturday, August 13, in the "greenish blue color" of the sun. According to Drewry, Turner the next day exhorted at a religious meeting of Negroes in the southern part of Southampton County (not in North Carolina as has been said) where some of the slaves "signified their willingness to co-operate with him by wearing around their necks red bandanna handkerchiefs." There was, certainly, a meeting of plotters in the afternoon of Sunday, August 21, and it was then decided to start the revolt that evening.

Appreciating the value of a dramatic entrance, Turner was the last to join this gathering. He noticed a newcomer in the group, and declared:

> I saluted them on coming up, and asked Will how came he there, he

answered, his life was worth no more than others, and his liberty as dear to him. I asked him if he meant to obtain it? He said he would, or loose his life. This was enough to put him in full confidence. . . .

The Revolt Erupts

These six slaves, then, started out, in the evening of August 21, 1831, on their crusade against bondage. Their first blow—delivered by Turner himself—struck against person and family of Turner's master, Joseph Travis, who were killed. Some arms and homes were taken, the rebels pushed on, and everywhere slaves flocked to their standard; a result which Turner, starting out with but a handful of followers, must have had excellent reasons to anticipate. Within twenty-four hours approximately seventy slaves were actively aiding in the rebellion. By the morning of August 23rd, at least fifty-seven whites—men, women, and children—had been killed, and the rebels had covered about twenty miles.

Turner declared that "indiscriminate slaughter was not their intention after they obtained a foothold, and was resorted to in the first instance to strike terror and alarm. Women and children would afterwards have been spared, and men too who ceased to resist." According to Governor John Floyd the slaves "spared but one family and that was one so wretched as to be in all respects upon a par with them."

In the morning of the twenty-third Turner and his followers set out for the county seat, Jerusalem, where there was a considerable store of arms. When about three miles from this town several of the slaves, notwithstanding Turner's objections, insisted upon trying to recruit the slaves of a wealthy planter named Parker. Turner, with a handful of followers, remained at the Parker gate while the rest went to the home itself, about half a mile away. Once at the Parker home many of the slaves appear to have slaked their thirst from its well-stocked cellar and to have rested. Turner became impatient and set out to get his tardy companions. The eight or nine slaves remaining at the gate were then attacked by a volunteer corps of whites of about twice their number. The slaves retreated, but upon being reinforced by the returning Turner and his men, the rebels pressed on and forced the whites to give ground. The latter, however, were in turn reinforced by a company of militia and the Negroes, whose guns, according to the Richmond *Compiler* of August 29, were not "fit for use," fled.

Though Turner later tried to round up sufficient followers to continue the struggle, his efforts were futile and this battle at Parker's field was the crucial one. Late in the day of this encounter the commander at Fort Monroe, Colonel Eustis, was requested by the Mayor of Norfolk to send aid. By the morning of the 24th, three companies of artillery with a field piece and one hundred stands of spare arms, together with detachments of men from the warships *Warren* and *Natchez* were on their way to the scene of the trouble. They made the sixty miles in one day, and met hundreds of other soldiers from volunteer and militia companies of the counties, in Virginia and in North Carolina, surrounding Southampton.

Massacre followed. Phillips simply notes, "a certain number of innocent blacks shot down," and Ballagh asserts, "A most impartial trial was given to all, except a few decapitated" in Southampton, while Drewry thought "there was far less of this indiscriminate murder than might have been expected." Just how much "indiscriminate murder" one ought to "expect" is not clear, but this statement by General Eppes, the officer in command of the affected county, leads one to believe that these historians were rather uncritical in dealing with this phase of the event:

> He [the General] will not specify all the instances that he is bound to believe have occurred, but pass in silence what has happened, with the expression of his deepest sorrow, that any necessity should be supposed to have existed, to justify a single act of atrocity. But he feels himself bound to declare, and hereby announces to the troops and citizens, that no excuse will be allowed for any similar acts of violence, after the promulgation of this order, and further to declare, in the most explicit terms, that any who may attempt the repetition of such acts, shall be punished, if necessary, by the rigors of the articles of war. The course that has been pursued, he fears, will in some instances be the means of rendering doubtful the guilt of those who may have participated in the carnage. . . . This course of proceeding dignified the rebel and the assassin with the sanctity of martyrdom, and confounds the difference that morality and religion makes between the ruffian and the brave and the honorable.

High Death Toll

The editor of the *Richmond Whig* also referred "with pain" to this "feature of the Southampton Rebellion. . . . We allude to the slaughter of many blacks without trial and under circumstances of great barbarity." He thought that about forty had thus been killed.

A Reverend G.W. Powell, writing August 27, when the reign of terror was by no means over, reported, "many negroes are killed every day. The exact number will never be known." The reverend gentleman was correct, but it appears certain that more, many more, than forty were massacred. The Huntsville, Alabama, *Southern Advocate* of October 15, 1831, declared that over one hundred Negroes had been killed in Southampton. It seems accurate to say that at least twice as many Negroes were indiscriminately slaughtered in that county, as the number of white people who had fallen victim to the vengeance and bondage-hating spirit of the slave.

That some considered themselves martyrs, as General Eppes suggested, is indicated by Governor Floyd's comment that "All died bravely indicating no reluctance to lose their lives in such a cause"; and a letter to Judge Thomas Ruffin of North Carolina declared, "some of them that were wounded and in the agonies of Death declared that they was going happy fore that God had a hand in what they had been doing."

Capture and Execution of Turner

Nat Turner eluded his pursuers from the end of August until October 30, when he was caught, armed only with an old sword, by Benjamin Phipps. During those weeks there had been rumors that he was caught, that he was a runaway in Maryland, that he was drowned, but as a matter of fact he never left his native county. He forsook his hiding place only at night for water, having supplied himself with food.

Turner was tried and, though pleading not guilty, since, as he said, he did not feel *guilty*, he was condemned to hang. The honorable Jeremiah Cobb pronounced sentence on November 5, in these words: "The judgement of the Court, is that you be taken hence to the jail from whence you came, thence to the place of execution, and on Friday next, between the hours of ten A.M. and 2 P.M. be hung by the neck until you are dead! dead! dead! and may the Lord have mercy upon your soul." About sixteen other slaves and three free Negroes had previously been executed, and on November the eleventh, 1831, their leader, the Prophet, he who had inspired them to value liberty above life, went calmly to his death. . . .

Panic in the Aftermath

With the news of this outbreak panic flashed through Virginia. The uprising was infectious and slaves everywhere became restless (or, at least, it was believed that they had become restless) so that the terror, momentarily localized in Virginia, spread up to Delaware and through Georgia, across to Louisiana and into Kentucky. This naturally led some to believe that Turner had concerted measures for rebellion over a wider area than his own county. Thus, Governor Floyd wrote: "From all that has come to my knowledge during and since this affair—I am fully convinced that every black preacher in the whole country east of the Blue Ridge, was in the secret," and again, "In relation to the extent of the insurrection I think it greater than will ever appear." A few other contemporary statements of similar purport appeared, and some later writers have adopted the same viewpoint.

The final authority on this question, however, is Nat Turner himself and he affirmed that the revolt he led was local, and that his activities had been confined to his own neighborhood. He added: "I see, sir, you doubt my word but can you not think the same ideas and strange appearances about this time in the heavens might prompt others, as well as myself, to this undertaking?" In the absence of any evidence of equal weight to the contrary, one must conclude that Turner possessed the characteristic of great leaders in that he sensed the mood and feelings of the masses of his fellow beings, not only in his immediate environment but generally. The years immediately preceding his effort had been marked by a great rumbling of discontent and protest. Turner's act, itself carrying that rumbling to a high point, caused an eruption throughout the length and breadth of the slave South—which always rested on a volcano of outraged humanity.

The *Richmond Enquirer* of August 26, 1831, while assuring the world that in its city there was "no disturbance, no suspicion, no panic," did note the fact that "a patrol turns out in our city every night." Two days later a resident of Richmond wrote to his New York friends that "the question now arises, if the slaves in that county, would murder the whites, whether they are not ready to do it in any other county in the State; and whether the reports that may spread among the slaves in other parts of the State, may not excite those to insurrection that never thought of such a thing before." Somewhat later, "A Friend of Precaution" wanted to know, "how can a remedy be provided? the safety of our wives and children, and their lives be preserved?"

These thoughts kept recurring and, together with the incessant stream of other slave plots and outbursts, developed a truly feverish state of mind. A niece of George Washington declared, "it is like a smothered volcano—we know not when, or where, the flame will burst forth but we know that death in the most horrid forms threaten us. Some have died, others have become deranged from apprehension since the South Hampton affair." And a gentleman in Virginia wrote to an acquaintance in Cincinnati:

> These insurrections have alarmed my wife so as really to endanger her health, and I have not slept without anxiety in three months. Our nights are sometimes spent in listening to noises. A corn song, or a hog call, has often been the subject of nervous terror, and a cat, in the dining room, will banish sleep for the night. There has been and there still is a *panic* in all this country. I am beginning to lose my courage about the melioration of the South. Our revivals produce no preachers; churches are like the buildings in which they worship, gone in a few years. There is no principle of life. Death is autocrat of slave regions.

The *Richmond Compiler* of September 3, 1831, contained this paragraph:

> Some rumors are still afloat; but we know not on what authority they rest, and we hope they are very much exaggerated; as, of a deposit of guns, pistols, and knives, being found in Nansemond—though a late letter from that county says all alarm had subsided. Yet we now and then hear of a suspected slave taken up in Nansemond and Surry—and we hear a report of a Patrol going upon an estate in Prince George and upon the overseer's pointing out five whom he suspected, shooting two who were attempting to escape, and securing the other three and throwing them into jail.

A little later were reported the convictions of about eleven slaves in the three eastern counties of Nansemond, Prince George, and Sussex. Then came the arrest and subsequent release of twelve in Norfolk, the conviction of one in Fredericksburg, and the jailing of forty more in Nansemond. Reports, no doubt greatly exaggerated, were current that two or three thousand Negroes were hiding in the Great Dismal Swamp, which extends from Southampton into North Carolina. The entire man-power of the State and much, if not all, its military might, infantry, artillery, cavalry, either in volunteer or regular militia units, were pressed into service throughout the Tidewater and the Piedmont areas, while the non-combatant population moved into garrisons, forts or blockhouses. Two slaves attempting to avoid arrest were shot and killed in Charles City County in September. The next month several slaves imprisoned in Sussex attempted to escape. One succeeded, one was killed, "another severely wounded—the remainder were secured without injury. On Friday [October 21] four of them were hung."

The Panic Spreads

The residents of Georgetown and Sussex, Delaware, and Easton and Seaford, Maryland, were panic-stricken, and slaves in those regions were arrested by the scores. Excitement in eastern North Carolina was as widespread and intense as in Virginia, indeed, it was so great that it led to the deaths of three white men, due to heart failure. Typical letters from this area told of the mobilization of the man-power, the need for more arms, the arrests of dozens of slaves, and the lashing or hanging of many. One from Murfrecsboro dated August 31, told of the arrest of five slaves, two of whom, London Gee and Sam Brantley, were supposed to be Baptist preachers. A show of force was still needed to convince the Negroes that revolt was hopeless. "Religion has been brought to their aid. Their leaders, who you know are preachers, have convinced many of them that to die in the cause in which they are engaged affords them a passport to heaven—many have said so when about to die." . . .

Heightened Security and New Legislation to Squash Rebellion

The basic idea represented by these communications, a stiffening and sharpening—once more—of the apparatus of suppression and terrorism, was instituted, following these [and other] outbreaks and plots of 1831, in city, state, and territory. This took, in the main, three forms: repression of the free Negro, repression of the slave, and attempts at the amelioration of the social unrest, resulting essentially in greater efforts at African colonization, and in the repression of anti-slavery opinion and thought in the South.

To exemplify the flood of legislation, two states, Maryland and Virginia, will be examined in detail. The General Assembly of Maryland meeting from December 1831 to March 1832 enacted the following pertinent laws. The immigration of free Negroes was forbidden. Any who did enter were not to be given employment, and if remaining over ten days were to pay fines of fifty dollars per week. No free Negro was to possess any weapons. Slaves and free Negroes were permitted to hold religious services only if whites were present. No foodstuff, tobacco, or spiritous liquors were to be bought from any Negro, nor were the latter to be sold to a Negro. The importation of slaves *for sale* after June 1, 1832, was forbidden. The Maryland State Colonization Society was incorporated and a Board of Managers, of three persons, was to be appointed by the Governor and Council. This Board was to spread propaganda detailing the alleged delights of Liberia, and to remove free Negros from the State. Twenty thousand dollars were given for 1831 and permission to subsequently borrow up to two hundred thousand dollars (the last sum was not "appropriated"). If not enough Negroes volunteered to leave to use up the available money, force was to be used. Moreover, the Congressmen from Maryland were memorialized to do what they could to obtain a grant from the federal government for colonization purposes, and if they deemed this unconstitutional to work for a constitutional amendment making the action possible, for "recent occurrences in this State, as well as in other states of our Union, have impressed more deeply upon our minds, the necessity of devising some means, by which we may facilitate the removal of the free persons of color from our state."

Though, as has been shown, Virginia passed many restrictive measures in the years immediately preceding Turner's revolt, her Assembly did find it possible to enact new regulations in the 1831–1832 meeting. It was then provided that "no slave, free negro, or mulatto, whether he shall have been ordained or licensed, or otherwise, shall hereafter undertake to preach, exhort, or conduct, or hold any assembly or meeting, for religious or other purposes, either in the day time, or at night," under a penalty of not over thirty-nine lashes. Whites, however, were allowed to take Negroes to their own services, and a licensed white preacher was permitted to address Negroes during the daytime. No free Negro was to possess weapons. If any Negro should commit assault on a white person with intent to kill, death without benefit of clergy was to be his punishment. No one was to sell liquor to or purchase it from a slave, and no Negro was to sell liquor within one mile of a public assembly. An act which went into operation July 1, 1832, provided that any Negro attending a seditious meeting or saying anything of such a nature was to be whipped not over thirty-nine times, while a white person so guilty was to be fined from one hundred to one thousand dollars. Another act, passed March 5,

1832, though as the influential editor Thomas Ritchie remarked, "applicable to one county only," was "deemed sufficiently important, (as affecting the general policy of the state,) to be inserted among the acts of a public nature." This provided that the fifteen thousand dollars pledged for the cause of colonization at a mass meeting in Northampton was to become part of the public debt of that county.

Questions Arise About Slavery Itself

But what this legislature did not do, and why; and what various citizens inside and outside the honorable body thought it ought to do, and what was said to and in, and reported about and asked of, this body are of greater significance than the laws it passed. In the twenties, with the prevailing depression, the acute fear of the Negroes, and the frequent manifestations of slave unrest, there had developed in the South, as has been indicated, a growing perplexity and doubt concerning the wisdom of slavery. Prior to the Turner rebellion this had been, on the whole, expressed in a hushed sort of way. Thus, Thomas Ritchie who, at least formally, was, prior to 1832, anti-slavery, urged western Virginians at the constitutional convention of 1829–30 to avoid emancipationist utterances.

The Turner cataclysm, however, succeeded in ripping up, for one year, the lid of censorship applied by the slaveocracy. This is especially true of the state most directly affected by that event, and the question of slavery was publicly debated for weeks in Virginia's legislature during the 1831–32 session. The western representatives, grieved at their section's inferior political position as compared with the east, and, restrained by no considerable body of slaveholding constituents, used antislavery utterances and sentiments—which were here expressed as deeply and as fully as they were ever to be in Ohio or Massachusetts—as a weapon in their sectional battle....

The decade of the twenties was a period of growth for the colonization movement, which was further accelerated by the Turner revolt. Some who became interested in it probably felt sincerely that it might end slavery. But, on the whole the purpose was to strengthen slavery by removing dangerous elements among the Negroes, keeping the growth of the free Negro population down, and confusing the anti-slavery movement.

EVENT 6

The Nat Turner Uprising: August 21–22, 1831

Turner's Account of the Uprising

by Nat Turner

Nat Turner was born on October 2, 1800, to a slave woman named Nancy. Turner's father fled during Turner's childhood, leaving his mother, a native of Africa, to rear the boy herself. A bright child who showed an early interest in religion, Turner was encouraged by his mother to regard himself as divinely chosen. Because he was better educated than many of his peers and he was an impassioned speaker, as an adult he easily fell into the role of leader among his fellow slaves. In 1830 he became the property of Joseph Travis and soon became a leader among the other slaves, convincing them early on that he was divinely inspired to lead them out of slavery.

He believed that he received divine guidance to revolt on August 21, 1831. After Turner's capture, the imprisoned slave calmly awaited execution. While in prison, he agreed to relate his account of the event to Thomas Gray, his assigned attorney.

Readers of the confession are generally shocked by Turner's matter-of-fact description of such a heinous murder spree. He provides a detailed house-by-house account of events, and expresses no remorse for his acts or his leadership of others to commit murder. Throughout the confession, he remains fully convinced that the uprising was morally right.

A greeable to his own appointment, on the evening he was committed to prison, with permission of the jailer, I visited NAT [Turner] on Tuesday the 1st November, when,

---

Nat Turner and Thomas Gray, "The Confessions of Nat Turner, the Leader of the Late Insurrection in Southampton, VA," *I Was Born a Slave: An Anthology of Classic Slave Narratives*, edited by Yuval Taylor. Vols. 1–2. Chicago: Lawrence Hill Books, 1999.

73

without being questioned at all, he commenced his narrative in the following words:—

Turner's Unusual Childhood

SIR,—You have asked me to give a history of the motives which induced me to undertake the late insurrection, as you call it—To do so I must go back to the days of my infancy, and even before I was born. I was thirty-one years of age the 2d of October last, and born the property of Benj. Turner, of this county. In my childhood a circumstance occurred which made an indelible impression on my mind, and laid the ground work of that enthusiasm, which has terminated so fatally to many, both white and black, and for which I am about to atone at the gallows. It is here necessary to relate this circumstance—trifling as it may seem, it was the commencement of that belief which has grown with time, and even now, sir, in this dungeon, helpless and forsaken as I am, I cannot divest myself of. Being at play with other children, when three or four years old, I was telling them something, which my mother overhearing, said it had happened before I was born—I stuck to my story, however, and related somethings which went, in her opinion, to confirm it—others being called on were greatly astonished, knowing that these things had happened, and caused them to say in my hearing, I surely would be a prophet, as the Lord had shewn me things that had happened before my birth. And my father and mother strengthened me in this my first impression, saying in my presence, I was intended for some great purpose, which they had always thought from certain marks on my head and breast—[a parcel of excrescences which I believe are not at all uncommon, particularly among negroes, as I have seen several with the same. In this case he has either cut them off or they have nearly disappeared]—My grandmother, who was very religious, and to whom I was much attached—my master, who belonged to the church, and other religious persons who visited the house, and whom I often saw at prayers, noticing the singularity of my manners, I suppose, and my uncommon intelligence for a child, remarked I had too much sense to be raised, and if I was, I would never be of any service to any one as a slave—To a mind like mine, restless, inquisitive and observant of every thing that was passing, it is easy to suppose that religion was the subject to which it would be directed, and although this subject principally occupied my thoughts—there was nothing that I saw or heard of to which my attention was not directed. . . .

Sense of Purpose and Leadership
Now finding I had arrived to man's estate [as a young man] and was a slave, and these revelations [of divine purpose] being made known to me. I began to direct my attention to this great object, to fulfil the purpose for which, by this time, I felt assured I was intended. Knowing the influence I had obtained over the minds of my fellow servants, (not by the means of conjuring and such like tricks—for to them I always spoke of such things with contempt) but by the communion of the Spirit whose revelations I often communicated to them, and they believed and said my wisdom came from God. I now began to prepare them for my purpose, by telling them something was about to happen that would terminate in fulfilling the great promise that had been made to me—About this time I was placed under an overseer, from whom I ran away—and after remaining in the woods thirty days, I returned, to the astonishment of the negroes on the plantation, who thought I had made my escape to some other part of the country, as my father had done before. But the reason of my return was, that the Spirit appeared to me and said I had my wishes directed to the things of this world, and not to the kingdom of Heaven, and that I should return to the service of my earthly master—"For he who knoweth his Master's will, and doeth it not, shall be beaten with many stripes, and thus have I chastened you." And the negroes found fault, and murmured against me, saying that if they had my sense they would not serve any master in the world. . . .

Turner Begins Plans for Uprising
And by signs in the heavens that it would make known to me when I should commence the great work—and until the first sign appeared, I should conceal it from the knowledge of men—And on the appearance of the sign, (the eclipse of the sun last February) I should arise and prepare myself, and slay my enemies with their own weapons. And immediately on the sign appearing in the heavens, the seal was removed from my lips, and I communicated the great work laid out for me to do, to four in whom I had the greatest confidence. (Henry, Hark, Nelson, and Sam)—It was intended by us to have begun the work of death on the 4th July last—Many were the plans formed and rejected by us, and it affected my mind to such a degree, that I fell sick, and the time passed without our coming to any determination how to commence—Still forming new schemes and rejecting them, when the

sign appeared again, which determined me not to wait longer.

Since the commencement of 1830, I had been living with Mr. Joseph Travis, who was to me a kind master, and placed the greatest confidence in me; in fact, I had no cause to complain of his treatment to me. On Saturday evening, the 20th of August, it was agreed between Henry, Hark and myself, to prepare a dinner the next day for the men we expected, and then to concert a plan, as we had not yet determined on any. Hark, on the following morning, brought a pig, and Henry brandy, and being joined by Sam, Nelson, Will and Jack, they prepared in the woods a dinner, where, about three o'clock, I joined them.

Q. Why were you so backward in joining them.

A. The same reason that had caused me not to mix with them for years before. [Turner had committed to spending more time in the spirit than with his fellow slaves.]

I saluted them on coming up, and asked Will how came he there, he answered, his life was worth no more than others, and his liberty as dear to him. I asked him if he thought to obtain it? He said he would, or loose his life. This was enough to put him in full confidence. Jack, I knew, was only a tool in the hands of Hark, it was quickly agreed we should commence at home (Mr. J. Travis') on that night, and until we had armed and equipped ourselves, and gathered sufficient force, neither age nor sex was to be spared, (which was invariably adhered to.) We remained at the feast, until about two hours in the night, when we went to the house and found Austin; they all went to the cider press and drank, except myself.

The Slaves Begin the Killing Spree

On returning to the house, Hark went to the door with an axe, for the purpose of breaking it open, as we knew we were strong enough to murder the family, if they were awaked by the noise; but reflecting that it might create an alarm in the neighborhood, we determined to enter the house secretly, and murder them whilst sleeping. Hark got a ladder and set it against the chimney, on which I ascended, and hoisting a window, entered and came down stairs, unbarred the door, and removed the guns from their places. It was then observed that I must spill the first blood. On which, armed with a hatchet, and accompanied by Will, I entered my master's chamber, it being dark, I could not give a death blow, the hatchet glanced from his head, he sprang from the bed and called his wife, it was his last word, Will laid him dead, with a blow of his axe, and Mrs. Travis shared the same fate, as she lay in bed. The murder of this family, five in number, was the work of a moment, not one of them awoke; there was a little infant sleeping in a cradle, that was forgotten, until we had left the house and gone some distance, when Henry and Will returned and killed it; we got here, four guns that would shoot, and several old muskets, with a pound or two of powder. We remained some time at the barn, where we paraded; I formed them in a line as soldiers, and after carrying them through all the manoevres I was master of, marched them off to Mr. Salathul Francis', about six hundred yards distant. Sam and Will went to the door and knocked. Mr. Francis asked who was there, Sam replied it was him, and he had a letter for him, on which he got up and came to the door; they immediately seized him, and dragging him out a little from the door, he was dis

Nat Turner led the 1831 slave revolt in Virginia. He was hanged twelve days after authorities captured him.

patched by repeated blows on the head; there was no other white person in the family. We started from there for Mrs. Reese's, maintaining the most perfect silence on our march, where finding the door unlocked, we entered, and murdured Mrs. Reese in her bed, while sleeping; her son awoke, but it was only to sleep the sleep of death, he had only time to say who is that, and he was no more. From Mrs. Reese's we went to Mrs. Turner's, a mile distant, which we reached about sunrise, on Monday morning. Henry, Austin, and Sam, went to the still, where, finding Mr. Peebles, Austin shot him, and the rest of us went to the house; as we approached, the family discovered us, and shut the door. Vain hope! Will, with one stroke of his axe, opened it, and we entered and found Mrs. Turner and Mrs. Newsome in the middle of a room, almost frightened to death. Will immediately killed Mrs. Turner, with one blow of his axe. I took Mrs. Newsome by the hand, and with the sword I had when I was apprehended, I struck her several blows over the head, but not being able to kill her, as the sword was dull. Will turning around and discovering it, despatched her also. A general destruction of property and search for money and ammunition, always succeeded the murders. By this time my company amounted to fifteen, and nine men mounted, who started for Mrs. Whitehead's, (the other six were to go through a by way to Mr. Bryant's, and rejoin us at Mrs. Whitehead's,) as we approached the house we discovered Mr. Richard Whitehead standing in the cotton patch, near the lane fence; we called him over into the lane, and Will, the executioner, was near at hand, with his fatal axe, to send him to an untimely grave. As we pushed on to the house, I discovered some one run round the garden, and thinking it was some of the white family, I pursued them, but finding it was a servant girl belonging to the house, I returned to commence the work of death, but they whom I left, had not been idle; all the family were already murdered, but Mrs. Whitehead and her daughter Margaret. As I came round to the door I saw Will pulling Mrs. Whitehead out of the house, and at the step he nearly severed her head from her body, with his broad axe. Miss Margaret, when I discovered her, had concealed herself in the corner, formed by the projection of the cellar cap from the house; on my approach she fled, but was soon overtaken, and after repeated blows with a sword, I killed her by a blow on the head, with a fence rail. By this time, the six who had gone by Mr. Bryant's, rejoined us, and informed me they had done the work of death assigned them. We again divided, part going to Mr. Richard Porter's, and from thence to Nathaniel Francis', the others to Mr. Howell Harris', and Mr. T. Doyles. On my reaching Mr. Porter's, he had escaped with his family. I understood there, that the alarm had already spread, and I immediately returned to bring up those sent to Mr. Doyles, and Mr. Howell Harris'; the party I left going on to Mr. Francis', having told them I would join them in that neighborhood. I met these sent to Mr. Doyles' and Mr. Harris' returning, having met Mr. Doyle on the road and killed him; and learning from some who joined them, that Mr. Harris was from home, I immediately pursued the course taken by the party gone on before; but knowing they would complete the work of death and pillage, at Mr. Francis' before I could get there, I went to Mr. Peter Edwards', expecting to find them there, but they had been here also. I then went to Mr. John T. Barrow's, they had been here and murdered him.

Turner's Group Grows in Number as the Killing Continues

I pursued on their track to Capt. Newit Harris', where I found the greater part mounted, and ready to start; the men now amounting to about forty, shouted and hurraed as I rode up, some were in the yard, loading their guns, others drinking. They said Captain Harris and his family had escaped, the property in the house they destroyed, robbing him of money and other valuables. I ordered them to mount and march instantly, this was about nine or ten o'clock, Monday morning. I proceeded to Mr. Levi Waller's, two or three miles distant. I took my station in the rear, and as it 'twas my object to carry terror and devastation wherever we went, I placed fifteen or twenty of the best armed and most to be relied on, in front, who generally approached the house as fast as their horses could run; this was for two purposes, to prevent their escape and strike terror to the inhabitants—on this account I never got to the houses, after leaving Mrs. Whitehead's, until the murders were committed, except in one case. I sometimes got in sight in time to see the work of death completed, viewed the mangled bodies as they lay, in silent satisfaction, and immediately started in quest of other victims—Having murdered Mrs. Waller and ten children, we started for Mr. William Williams'—having killed him and two little boys that were there; while engaged in this, Mrs. Williams fled and got some distance from the house, but she was pursued, overtaken, and compelled to get up behind one of the company, who brought her back, and after showing her the mangled body of her lifeless husband, she was told to get down and lay by his side, where she was shot dead. I then started for Mr. Jacob Williams, where the family were murdered—Here we found a young man named Drury, who had come on business with Mr. Williams—he was pursued, overtaken and shot. Mrs. Vaughan was the next place we visited—and after murdering the family here, I determined on starting for Jerusalem—Our number amounted now to fifty or sixty, all mounted and armed with guns, axes, swords and clubs—On reaching Mr. James W. Parkers' gate, immediately on the road leading to Jerusalem, and about three miles distant, it was proposed to me to call there, but I objected, as I knew he was gone to Jerusalem, and my object was to reach there as soon as possible; but some of the men having relations at Mr. Parker's it was agreed that they might call and get his people.

The Uprising Is Finally Stopped by Force

I remained at the gate on the road, with seven or eight; the others going across the field to the house, about half a mile off. After waiting some time for them, I became impatient, and started to the house for them, and on our return we were met by a party of white men, who had pursued our blood-stained track, and who had fired on those at the gate, and dispersed them, which I new nothing of, not having been at that time rejoined by any of them —Immediately on discovering the whites, I ordered my men to halt and form, as they appeared to be alarmed—The white men, eighteen in number, approached us in about one hundred yards, when one of them fired, (this was against the positive orders of Captain Alexander P. Peete, who commanded, and who had directed the men to reserve their fire until within thirty paces). And I discovered about half of them retreating, I then ordered my men to fire and rush on them; the few remaining stood their ground until we approached within fifty yards, when they fired and retreated. We pursued and overtook some of them who we thought we left dead; (they were not killed) after pursuing them about two hundred yards, and rising a little hill, I discovered they were met by another party, and had haulted, and were re-loading their guns, (this was a small party from Jerusalem who knew the negroes were in the field, and had just tied their horses to await their return to the road, knowing that Mr. Parker and family were in Jerusalem, but knew nothing of the party that had gone in with Captain Peete; on hearing the firing they immediately rushed to the spot and arrived just in time to arrest the progress of these barbarous villians, and save the lives of their friends and fellow citizens.) Thinking that those who retreated first, and the party who fired on us at fifty or sixty yards distant, had all only fallen back to meet others with amunition. As I saw them reloading their guns, and more coming up than I saw at first, and several of my bravest men being wounded, the others became panic struck and squandered over the field; the white men pursued and fired on us several times.

Turner Flees with a Smaller Group

Hark had his horse shot under him, and I caught another for him as it was running by me; five or six of my men were wounded, but none left on the field; finding myself defeated here I instantly determined to go through a private way, and cross the Nottoway river at the Cypress Bridge, three miles below Jerusalem, and attack that place in the rear, as I expected they would look for me on the other road, and I had a great desire to get there to procure arms and amunition. After going a short distance in this private way, accompanied by about twenty men, I overtook two or three who told me the others were dispersed in every direction. After trying in vain to collect a sufficient force to proceed to Jerusalem, I determined to return, as I was sure they would make back to their old neighborhood, where they would rejoin me, make new recruits, and come down again. On my way back, I called at Mrs. Thomas's, Mrs. Spencer's, and several other places, the white families having fled, we found no more victims to gratify our thirst for blood, we stopped at Majr. Ridley's quarter for the night, and being joined by four of his men, with the recruits made since my defeat, we mustered now about forty strong. After placing out sentinels, I laid down to sleep, but was quickly roused by a great racket; starting up, I found some mounted, and others in great confusion; one of the sentinels having given the alarm that we were about to be attacked, I ordered some to ride round and reconnoitre, and on their return the others being more alarmed, not knowing who they were, fled in different ways, so that I was reduced to about twenty again; with this I determined to attempt to recruit, and proceed on to rally in the neighborhood, I had left. Dr. Blunt's was the nearest house, which we reached just before day; on riding up the yard, Hark fired a gun. We expected Dr. Blunt and his family were at Maj. Ridley's, as I knew there was a company of men there; the gun was fired to ascertain if any of the family were at home; we were immediately fired upon and retreated, leaving several of my men. I do not know what became of them, as I never saw them afterwards. Pursuing our course back and coming in sight of Captain Harris', where we had been the day before, we discovered a party of white men at the house, on which all deserted me but two, (Jacob and Nat,) we concealed ourselves in the woods until near night, when I sent them in search of Henry, Sam, Nelson, and Hark, and directed them to rally all they could, at the place we had had our dinner the Sunday before, where they would find me, and I accordingly returned there as soon as it was dark and remained until Wednesday evening, when discovering white men riding around the place as though they were looking for some one, and none of my men joining me, I concluded Jacob and Nat had been taken, and compelled to betray me.

Turner Goes into Hiding Alone and Is Caught

On this I gave up all hope for the present; and on Thursday night after having supplied myself with provisions from Mr. Travis's, I scratched a hole under a pile of fence rails in a field, where I concealed myself for six weeks, never leaving my hiding place but for a few minutes in the dead of night to get water which was very near; thinking by this time I could venture out, I began to go about in the night and eaves drop the houses in the neighborhood; pursuing this course for about a fortnight and gathering little or no intelligence, afraid of speaking to any human being, and returning every morning to my cave before the dawn of day. I know not how long I might have led this life, if accident had not betrayed me, a dog in the neighborhood passing by my hiding place one night while I was out, was attracted by some meat I had in my cave, and crawled in and stole it, and was coming out just as I returned. A few nights after, two negroes having started to go hunting with the same dog, and passed that way, the dog came again to the place, and having just gone out to walk about, discovered me and barked, on which thinking myself discovered, I spoke to them to beg concealment. On making myself known they fled from me. Knowing then they would betray me, I immediately left my hiding place, and was pursued almost incessantly until I was taken a fortnight afterwards by Mr. Benjamin Phipps, in a little hole I had dug out with my sword, for the purpose of concealment, under the top of a fallen tree. On Mr. Phipps' discovering the place of my concealment, he cocked his gun and aimed at me. I requested him not to shoot and I would give up, upon which he demanded my sword. I delivered it to him, and he brought me to prison. During the time I was pursued, I had many hair breadth escapes, which your time will not permit you to relate. I am here loaded with chains, and willing to suffer the fate that awaits me.

EVENT 7 The Treaty of London: May 7, 1832

Greek Nationalism Is Finally Rewarded with Independence

by Augustus Oakes and R.B. Mowat

Greece's history as the home of democracy fueled its nineteenth-century drive to free itself from four centuries of Turkish rule. In the 1820s, the first outbreaks of revolution occurred. Without outside help, however, the prospect of independence seemed unlikely.

Most Europeans supported the idea of Greek independence, and as leadership of powerful nations changed hands, more practical aid to the Greeks was planned. Together, Great Britain, France, and Russia rallied to Greece's side, and after defeating the Turks at the Battle of Navarino, the three European nations signed the 1827 Treaty of London, granting Greece its much-anticipated independence.

The following article explains the conditions of Turkish rule in Greece and the steps taken by Great Britain, France, and Russia to aid the Greek nationalist cause. It also reviews the significance of the terms of the 1832 treaty. The full text of the treaty is also presented to give the full historical perspective.

Authors Sir Augustus Oakes worked in the British government, and R.B. Mowat is a professor at Corpus Christi College in Oxford.

Augustus Oakes and R.B. Mowat, eds., *The Great European Treaties of the Nineteenth Century*. Oxford, UK: Clarendon, 1918.

THE TREATY OF LONDON

For thirty-three years after the Congress of Vienna, the peace of Europe, though often threatened, was never seriously disturbed. This was partly due to the aversion from war left upon men's minds by the memory of the sanguinary period which had been ushered in by the French Revolution; partly also to the efforts of the Holy Alliance [an alliance of European leaders committed to Christianity in their rule] to maintain the peace of Europe by concerted action of the Powers. But the policy of the Holy Alliance could not be maintained against the growing sentiment of nationalism, which by the year 1820 was showing itself to be a potent force in Spain, Italy, and in Greece. It was in the latter country that nationalism attained one of its earliest and most remarkable developments in the nineteenth century.

Greece, since the great days of the fifth century before Christ, had passed through many vicissitudes. In turn, Romans, Byzantines, and crusading Franks had held it. Italians from Naples, Florence, and Venice had left their mark in Attica and the Morea. But by 1460 the whole of Greece had come under the Turks, whose dominion over it, except for eighteen years of Venetian government in the Morea (1699 to 1718), remained unbroken till the nineteenth century had run one-quarter of its course.

In the meantime, during the Middle Ages and the later centuries, the Greeks had not preserved the ancient purity of their race. The Slavs had come down south of the Balkans, and the Albanians had penetrated as far even as Attica. The Greek language had become degraded into patois, filled with alien words; the glorious classics of ancient Greece were forgotten in the land.

But in the hundred years before the War of Independence actually broke out, forces were at work which gradually wrought upon the modern Greeks the consciousness that they were the heirs of an ancient heritage, that they were a people fitted still to be free and independent.

This growth of a national sentiment was not the result of Turkish misgovernment. The Turks have indeed never been good administrators. Their financial and judicial systems in Greece were in certain directions oppressive owing to an arbitrary and corrupt element in them. Yet the Turks, like all arbitrary but ill-organized governments, left a considerable amount of freedom to their subjects, and the Greeks under their rule enjoyed a considerable share of prosperity. This prosperity was noticeable throughout the whole of the eighteenth century. The peasantry either cultivated their own land, or held it as tenants, paying a fixed amount of the produce as rent. Their social and economic condition was good: 'in comparison with the Prussian serf, the Greek cultivator at the beginning of the eighteenth century was an independent man; in comparison with the English labourer, he was well fed and well housed.' Their prosperous condition made them receptive of other influences which tended to a spiritual awakening. There were, moreover, sufficient sources of irritation in the Turkish régime to make the Greeks look upon their conquerors as infidel oppressors.

Greek Society Under Turkish Rule

The Greek Church had always kept alive a certain amount of national feeling. The lower clergy were men of the people, married, very little above the level of those whose spiritual needs they tended. They were superstitious and unlearned, but had not the less on this account the sympathy of their flock. The higher clergy, the bishops, belonged to the monastic side of the Church; they, too, had considerable influence over the people, through the bishops' courts, where the Turks permitted cases of both spiritual and secular interest to be brought. The services of the Church preserved something more of the classical Greek language than was contained in the vernacular of the country.

Under the Turkish régime there was almost an official aristocracy of Greeks—wealthy families, dwelling in the quarter of Constantinople by the Phanar lighthouse. These 'Phanariot' Greeks regularly held important appointments in the Turkish administration, such as that side of it which dealt with foreign relations, with the drafting of treaties, and such matters. Moreover, since the end of the native tributary princes of Wallachia and of Moldavia between 1711 and 1716, the Phanariot Greeks had by purchase secured the 'farm' of the governorship of the Principalities. The Phanariots were well-educated and often able men, who did much by establishing schools to spread the feeling of Hellenism throughout their countrymen. In this work, at the end of the eighteenth century, they were much helped by wealthy Greeks who had established themselves in Odessa, a city which was founded by the Russians in 1790, and where Greek merchants established a great hold upon the corntrade.

The one man who did more than any other to train and develop the comparatively small germ of national feeling which existed before his time among the Greeks was Adamantos Coräes, who devoted his long life to re-creating Greek literature and spreading the knowledge of the ancient Hellenic classics. This great scholar lived from the year 1748 to 1833, and from the year 1789 resided at Paris, an observer of the French Revolution and of the reverberations of that remarkable event in Western Europe. Spiritual things are more potent than material, and it is impossible to overestimate the effect of the scholarship of Coräes. Expensive editions of Homer and Aristotle may not appear at first sight to be the best means of rousing an ignorant and half-Slavonic people to a sense of community with the free ancient Greeks whose language they did not understand. But Greek studies had never been really dead among the Phanariots at anytime in the eighteenth century. Coräes had something to build upon, and gradually he not merely extended the knowledge of ancient Greek literature, with all the political ideals that it contained, but he also created a literary language for the modern Greeks, a vehicle for the transmission of knowledge, purer than the debased patois of the peasants, but not so archaic as to be unsuitable for the needs of modern men.

Revolutionary Stirrings and Early Outbreaks

By the end of the Napoleonic Wars, Greece was ready to revolt. There was a large mercantile marine, manned by the hardy islanders of the Aegean, sailing largely under the Russian flag, monopolizing a great part of the commerce of the Black Sea and the Levant. The powerful secret society, the Hetaeria Philikë, founded by the wealthy enlightened Greeks of Odessa in 1814, did much to spread the seeds of revolt. In 1820 Alexander Ypsilanti, who belonged to a distinguished Phanariot family, and had risen to be a major-general in the service of the Tsar Alexander I, was elected president of the Hetaeria Philikë.

Next year, March 6, 1821, he crossed the Pruth with his following of Greek officers from the Russian service. The revolt was ill-timed and ill-conducted. Some temporary success was attained in the Principalities, but before June was out the Turks had driven him across the frontier into Austrian territory, where he was imprisoned for the next seven years, and then released to die in poverty. The revolt was thus suppressed in Wallachia and Moldavia, but it broke out simultaneously in the Morea and soon spread throughout all Greece. But it had no great success for some years yet. For when the Porte had succeeded in subduing their rebellious Pasha, Ali of Yanina, their forces were too much for the divided, ill-organized Greeks. Nor did the Powers of Europe give them any encouragement or support.

For five years war went on without any decisive result. The peasant-soldiers of the Greek mainland and the hardy islanders by sea proved themselves to be good fighters. Yet the war was not more creditable to the Greeks than to the Turks; it became a war of religion and of race, disgraced by terrible massacres on either side. The Greeks themselves could not agree, and at times there was open civil war among them.

Europe Rallies to Greece's Cause

The public opinion of Europe was in favour of the Greek national cause, but the Governments at first were against it. In 1821 Castlereagh still directed British foreign policy, and was anxious to maintain the existing state of affairs fearful of another general conflagration such as Europe had passed through after the French Revolution. Metternich was still the guiding spirit of the Holy Alliance, and prevented Alexander I of Russia from giving support to the Greeks.

In 1822 Castlereagh died by his own hand, and was succeeded as Foreign Secretary by the liberal-minded Canning. British volunteers, such as the poet Byron, the soldier Church, the sailor Cochrane, who in their different ways gave most valuable help, joined themselves to the Greek cause. Yet the year 1825 closed with the Greek cause standing lower than ever, for Sultan Mahmud had called in the support of his independent Pasha, Mehemet Ali of Egypt, whose able son Ibrahim reconquered the Morea. The British Government had felt bound to prohibit its subjects from taking any part in the war. But at the end of the year (December 1, 1825) Tsar Alexander I of Russia died, giving place to his younger brother, the determined and energetic Nicholas I, who gradually and in the end decisively made his influence felt upon the destinies of Greece.

The Tsar Nicholas was no democrat, but as the head of Russia his interests lay in striking at Turkish power in Europe, and in helping the Orthodox Greek subjects of the Porte. Canning, unlike Nicholas, was both liberal-minded and the inheritor of a tradition, then just becoming firmly established, of friendship with Turkey and support of Turkey in Europe. Yet he had sympathy with national ideals and with Greek aspirations, and the public opinion of England was with him. He decided to approach Nicholas, and accordingly in 1826 sent the Duke of Wellington to Petrograd. The Duke, a strong Conservative, a firm upholder of constituted authority, had no liking for a mission in favour of the rebel Greeks. Yet when asked to go to Petrograd, his simple creed of duty admitted of no alternative. Once he made up his mind to carry out the mission, no man was better fitted for it. His character was naturally congenial to Nicholas, and it did not take them long to come to an understanding. On April 4, 1826, the Protocol of St. Petersburg was signed.

By this arrangement Great Britain and Russia agreed to offer their mediation to the Porte with a view to placing Greece in the position of a Dependency of Turkey. The Greeks 'should pay to the Porte an annual Tribute', and 'should be exclusively governed by authorities to be chosen and named by themselves, but in the nomination of which authorities the Porte should have a certain influence'. If the Porte should reject the proffered mediation, Great Britain and Russia were still to consider this scheme as the basis of any settlement 'to be effected by their intervention, whether in concert or separately'.

Next year France gave its adhesion to the policy laid down in the Protocol of St. Petersburg. On July 6, 1827, the three countries concluded a formal treaty embodying the provisions of that document. To this were added some important clauses. If the Turks refused the mediation the Allies would take steps to recognize Greek independence by appointing consular agents to Greece. If neither side would agree to an armistice, the Allies would take steps to prevent a collision between them, 'without, however, taking any part in the hostilities between the Two Contending Parties'.

The [1827] Treaty of London was Canning's last achievement. He had only become Prime Minister, in succession to the venerable Earl of Liverpool, in April. In August he himself died. Lord Goderich became Prime Minister. It was during this statesman's term of office that the momentous battle of Navarino occurred.

The Battle of Navarino and War with Turkey

An armistice had been proposed to the belligerents; this the Greeks had, naturally, accepted readily, but the Turks had refused. Accordingly the Allied admirals in the Mediterranean, in accordance with their instructions, resolved to put pressure on the Porte. On

October 20 the English, French, and Russian squadrons sailed into the Bay of Navarino, the ancient Pylus, on the south-east coast of the Morea. The object of the admirals was to parley with the Turkish commander and to persuade him to an armistice. The Turkish chief, Ibrahim Pasha, was at the time away with his land forces, devastating the Morea. The colloquy with the Turks in Navarino Bay ended, as it was practically certain to do, with hostile acts on the part of the Turkish captains. The Allied fleet was in battle order, ready for such an emergency. A general conflict ensued, and by the end of the day the Egyptian fleet was destroyed.

This great battle saved Greece, for although the mainland was now overrun by the Turks, they could not touch the Islands, the real strongholds of the Greek cause. Yet its immediate results were disappointing. Admiral Codrington, who as senior officer was in command of the Allied fleet, wished to force the Dardanelles (then quite a feasible operation), and by appearing off Constantinople, to compel the Porte to accept the Treaty of London. But Canning's vigorous hand was no longer at the helm of the ship of Lord Goderich resigned. The Duke of Wellington became Prime Minister, resolved that he would intervene no further. The inaction of Britain, however, made very little difference to Greece now; it only meant that Russia would gain the laurels which Britain should have shared with her. On April 20, 1828, Tsar Nicholas began war upon Turkey. The campaign of this year was a failure, but in 1829 the soldierly qualities of Diebitsch quickly made themselves felt. The passage of the Balkans was forced, and on September 14 the Porte accepted terms of peace at Adrianople. By Article X of this treaty Turkey agreed to adhere to the Treaty of London, 1827, in which Great Britain, Russia, and France defined their scheme for the settlement of Greece.

The 1832 Treaty of London Secures Greek Independence

The independence of Greece was thus achieved. While the Russians had been fighting in Bulgaria, the Greeks in the Morea, aided by a French expedition sent in 1828, had reconquered that region. On February 3, 1830, the three Powers, Great Britain, France, and Russia, by a protocol entered into at London, carried into effect the declared intention of their Treaty of 1827. The Porte, by Article X of the Treaty of Adrianople, had agreed to such a course of action on the part of the Powers. But the Protocol of 1830 secured to Greece far better terms than the Treaty of 1827 had outlined, for in the interval the Turks had been defeated by land and sea, had lost the whole of Greece south of the Gulf of Corinth and a considerable tract to the north of the Gulf, and had been faced with the prospect of seeing a Russian army before the walls of Constantinople. Their chance of keeping the Greeks tributary had therefore passed away. The Protocol of London, 1830, declared Greece to be a completely independent State. It was to be a monarchy, under a Sovereign Prince, who should not be a member of the reigning families of any of the Powers signatory of the Treaty of 1827. Since 1827 the President of the Greek Government had been the able and patriotic Capodistrias. On February 11, 1830, the crown was accepted by Leopold of Saxe-Coburg (subsequently King Leopold I of Belgium), but he never came to his adopted country, for he renounced it in May of the same year. Capodistrias therefore remained President, but was himself assassinated in October 1831. His death was followed by another troubled period in Greece, till on May 7, 1832, the three Powers made their final act, the well-known Treaty of London, which definitely secured Greek independence, on a substantial footing.

Terms of the Treaty

The preamble to this treaty refers to the desire which the Greek leaders had on various occasions expressed to the three Powers that they would intervene to effect a settlement between Greece and Turkey. The Turks, naturally, had refused such mediation, as long as their arms were successful. But the battle of Navarino and the campaign of General Diebitsch had put an end to the Turks' chances of subduing Greece, and this they had definitely recognized when they concluded the Treaty of Adrianople. The Protocol of London, 1830, had made Greece independent under the guarantee of the three Powers, and is referred to in Articles IV and VI of the 1832 Treaty. The Treaty of 1827 had declared that Greece should be tributary to Turkey: the Turks refused this. The Protocol of 1830 had declared that Greece should be independent under a Sovereign Prince. Finally, the 1832 Treaty made Greece a kingdom.

By Article I the crown was offered to a prince of the ancient House of Wittelsbach, Frederick Otho, second son of King Ludwig I of Bavaria. Article IV placed the independence of Greece under the guarantee of Great Britain, France, and Russia; this guarantee is referred to and continued in the Treaty of London, July 13, 1863. Article V leaves the Greek boundaries to be settled by negotiations which were then going on between the three Powers and Turkey. Article VIII contains the stipulation, usual in treaties regarding the establishment of a dynasty belonging to an already reigning house, that the two crowns are never to be united. Three other points of permanent interest appear in the treaty: by Article XII the three Powers engaged, the Emperor of Russia by his autocratic power, Great Britain and France with the consent of their legislative bodies, to guarantee the interest and sinking fund of a loan to be raised by Greece. Article XIII refers to a pecuniary indemnity to Turkey, for loss of territory owing to the establishment of Greek independence. Articles XIV and XV declared that a small body of troops and officers should be brought from Bavaria to Greece, to assist in its organization.

Under the conditions of Article XII Greece raised a loan of 60,000,000 francs; in 1857, owing to the failure of the Greek Government to meet the charges for interest and sinking fund, Great Britain, France, and Russia had to supply the necessary funds. In 1860 an arrangement was come to by which Greece should begin again to contribute towards the discharge of her obligations, by paying £12,000 per annum to each of the three Powers, who were discharging her loan. This arrangement is still in force, but, during the lifetime of King George, the three Powers, under the Treaty of March 29, 1864; annually gave back £4,000 each as an addition to the Civil List of the Greek Crown.

The indemnity referred to in Article XIII was fixed at 40,000,000 *piastres*, in the boundary treaty between Great Britain, France, and Russia on the one part, and Turkey on the other, concluded on July 21, 1832. This sum, equal to about £375,000, was not of course compensation to Turkey for the loss of Greece, but for losses due to individual landed proprietors. . . .

Text of the 1832 Treaty of London

CONVENTION BETWEEN GREAT BRITAIN, FRANCE, AND RUSSIA, ON THE ONE PART, AND BAVARIA ON THE OTHER, RELATIVE TO THE SOVEREIGNTY OF GREECE. SIGNED AT LONDON, 7TH MAY, 1832.

ARTICLE I. The Courts of Great Britain, France, and Russia, duly authorised for this purpose by the Greek nation, offer the hereditary Sovereignty of Greece to the Prince Frederick Otho of

Bavaria, second son of His Majesty the King of Bavaria.

ARTICLE II. His Majesty the King of Bavaria, acting in the name of his said son, a minor, accepts, on his behalf, the hereditary Sovereignty of Greece, on the conditions hereinafter settled.

ARTICLE III. The Prince Otho of Bavaria shall bear the title of King of Greece.

ARTICLE IV. Greece, under the Sovereignty of the Prince Otho of Bavaria, and under the Guarantee of the 3 Courts, shall form a monarchical and independent State, according to the terms of the Protocol signed between the said Courts on the 3rd February, 1830, and accepted both by Greece and by the Ottoman Porte.

ARTICLE V. The limits of the Greek State shall be such as shall be definitively settled by the negotiations which the Courts of Great Britain, France, and Russia have recently opened with the Ottoman Porte, in execution of the Protocol of 26th of September, 1831.

ARTICLE VI. The 3 Courts having beforehand determined to convert the Protocol of the 3rd of February, 1830 into a Definitive Treaty, as soon as the negotiations relative to the limits of Greece shall have terminated, and to communicate such Treaty to all the States with which they have relations, it is hereby agreed that they shall fulfil this engagement, and that His Majesty the King of Greece shall become a Contracting Party to the Treaty in question.

ARTICLE VII. The 3 Courts shall, from the present moment, use their influence to procure the recognition of the Prince Otho of Bavaria as King of Greece, by all the Sovereigns and States with whom they have relations.

ARTICLE VIII. The Royal Crown and dignity shall be hereditary in Greece; and shall pass to the direct and lawful descendants and heirs of the Prince Otho of Bavaria, in the order of primogeniture. In the event of the decease of the Prince Otho of Bavaria, without direct and lawful issue, the Crown of Greece shall pass to his younger brother, and to his direct and lawful descendants and heirs, in the order of primogeniture. In the event of the decease of the last-mentioned Prince also, without direct and lawful issue, the Crown of Greece shall pass to his younger brother, and to his direct and lawful descendants and heirs, in the order of primogeniture.

In no case shall the Crown of Greece and the Crown of Bavaria be united upon the same head.

ARTICLE IX. The majority of the Prince Otho of Bavaria, as King of Greece, is fixed at the period when he shall have completed his 20th year, that is to say, on the 1st of June, 1835.

ARTICLE X. During the minority of the Prince Otho of Bavaria, King of Greece, his rights of Sovereignty shall be exercised in their full extent, by a Regency composed of 3 Councillors, who shall be appointed by His Majesty the King of Bavaria.

ARTICLE XI. The Prince Otho of Bavaria shall retain the full possession of his appanages in Bavaria. His Majesty the King of Bavaria, moreover, engages to assist, as far as may be in his power, the Prince Otho in his position in Greece, until a revenue shall have been set apart for the Crown in that State.

ARTICLE XII. In execution of the Stipulations of the Protocol of the 20th of February, 1830, His Majesty the Emperor of All the Russias engages to guarantee, and their Majesties the King of the United Kingdom of Great Britain and Ireland, and the King of the French, engage to recommend, the former to his Parliament, and the latter to his Chambers, to enable their Majesties to guarantee, on the following conditions, a Loan to be contracted by the Prince Otho of Bavaria, as King of Greece.

1. The principal of the Loan to be contracted under the guarantee of the 3 Powers, shall not exceed a total amount of 60,000,000 of francs.

2. The said Loan shall be raised by instalments of 20,000,000 of francs each.

3. For the present, the first instalment only shall be raised, and the 3 Courts shall each become responsible for the payment of one-third of the annual amount of the interest and sinking fund of the said instalment.

4. The second and the third instalments of the said Loan may also be raised, according to the necessities of the Greek State, after previous agreement between the Courts and His Majesty the King of Greece.

5. In the event of the second and third instalments of the abovementioned Loan being raised in consequence of such an agreement, the 3 Courts shall each become responsible for the payment of one-third of the annual amount of the interest and sinking fund of these two instalments, as well as of the first.

6. The Sovereign of Greece and the Greek State shall be bound to appropriate to the payment of the interest and sinking fund, of such instalments of the Loan as may have been raised under the guarantee of the 3 Courts, the first revenues of the State, in such manner that the actual receipts of the Greek Treasury shall be de-

voted, *first of all*, to the payment of the said interest and sinking fund, and shall not be employed for any other purpose until those payments on account of the instalments of the Loan raised under the guarantee of the 3 Courts shall have been completely secured for the current year.

The diplomatic Representatives of the 3 Courts in Greece shall be specially charged to watch over the fulfilment of the last-mentioned stipulation.

ARTICLE XIII. In case a pecuniary compensation in favour of the Ottoman Porte should result from the negotiations which the 3 Courts have already opened at Constantinople for the definitive settlement of the limits of Greece, it is understood that the amount of such compensation shall be defrayed out of the proceeds of the Loan which forms the subject of the preceding Article.

ARTICLE XIV. His Majesty the King of Bavaria shall lend his assistance to the Prince Otho in raising in Bavaria a body of troops, not exceeding 3,500 men, to be employed in his service, as King of Greece, which corps shall be armed, equipped, and paid by the Greek State, and be sent thither as soon as possible, in order to relieve the troops of the Alliance hitherto stationed in Greece. The latter shall remain in that country entirely at the disposal of the Government of His Majesty the King of Greece, until the arrival of the body of troops above mentioned. Immediately upon their arrival the troops of the Alliance already referred to shall retire, and altogether evacuate the Greek territory.

ARTICLE XV. His Majesty the King of Bavaria shall also assist the Prince Otho in obtaining the services of a certain number of Bavarian officers, who shall organize a national military force in Greece.

ARTICLE XVI. As soon as possible after the signature of the present Convention, the 3 Councillors who are to be associated with His Royal Highness the Prince Otho by His Majesty the King of Bavaria, in order to compose the Regency of Greece, shall repair to Greece, shall enter upon the exercise of the functions of the said Regency, and shall prepare all the measures necessary for the reception of the Sovereign, who, on his part, will repair to Greece with as little delay as possible.

ARTICLE XVII. The 3 Courts shall announce to the Greek nation, by a joint declaration, the choice which they have made of His Royal Highness Prince Otho of Bavaria, as King of Greece, and shall afford the Regency all the support in their power.

ARTICLE XVIII. The present Convention shall be ratified, and the Ratifications shall be exchanged at London in 6 weeks, or sooner if possible. In witness whereof the respective Plenipotentiaries have signed the same, and have affixed thereto the Seal of their Arms. Done at London, the 7th May, in the year of Our Lord, 1832.
    (L.S.) PALMERSTON.
    (L.S.) TALLEYRAND.
    (L.S.) LIEVEN.
    (L.S.) MATUSZEWIC.
    (L.S.) A. DE COTTO.

EVENT 8 The Coronation of Queen Victoria: June 28, 1838

The Legacy of Queen Victoria's Reign

by Lynne Vallone

Victorian England is fondly remembered as a golden age. At the center of the Victorian age is Queen Victoria herself. Despite early attempts to control and manipulate her (even before she became queen), she proved a strong, independent, and insightful monarch who was respected by world leaders and generally loved by the English people. To protect herself and her country, she sought only what she considered wise political counsel, while carefully navigating the rough terrain of diplomacy. During her long reign, she oversaw Britain's rise to world leadership in science, industry, and the arts. As a strong woman with a large family and an active role in the governing of her nation, Victoria was a unique figure in British history. Despite accusations of foot-dragging in social reform, she was a beloved figure.

The following discussion of Victoria's reign explains the expectations that young Victoria faced and how she refused to be guided by them. Author Lynne Vallone describes the strong, independent personality that characterized Victoria's public self and the more vulnerable private self that only her family saw. Throughout, Vallone explains how influential Victoria's reign was to Britain at the time and even today. Vallone is a professor of English at Texas A&M University who, along with an interest in Queen Victoria, specializes in children's literature and nineteenth-century women's literature.

Lynne Vallone, "Victoria: Lynne Vallone Reviews the Life of the Woman Who Has Occupied the Throne Longer than Any Other Individual and Considers the Tensions Between Her Private and Public Selves," *History Today*, vol. 52, June 2002, pp. 46–53. Copyright © 2002 by History Today, Ltd. Reproduced by permission.

As a symbol of domesticity, endurance and Empire, and as a woman holding the highest public office during an age when women (middle-class women, at least) were expected to beautify the home while men dominated the public sphere, Queen Victoria's influence has been enduring. The historian Dorothy Thompson (1990) suggests that the present queen has extended and emphasised the tenets and trends of Victoria's reign to the present day.

The symbolic importance of Victoria's reign (1837–1901) cannot easily be separated from assumptions made by her contemporaries about gender and age. Adjectives such as 'simple', 'modest', 'innocent', 'lovely', commonly applied to Victoria as evidence of her appropriate placement on the throne, would almost certainly not have been used if she had been a man. Similarly, after her death from old age in January, 1901, paeans to the Queen praised her embodiment of traditional feminine virtues rather than acts of bravery, statesmanship, or guardianship. For example, best-selling novelist Marie Corelli, in *The Passing of the Great Queen: A Tribute to the Noble Life of Victoria Regina* (1901), prefers Victoria's model of 'blameless' feminine authority to masculine privilege. Corelli remarks that

> Personal influence is a far more important factor in the welding together and holding of countries and peoples than is generally taken into account by such of us are superficial observers and who imagine that everything is done by Governments.

Conflicts between the demands of 'masculine' government and 'feminine' home are located within the person of the woman who was from 1837 until her death sixty-three years later, at the head of both. Although she would later express a horror of women's rights, the Queen articulated a clearly-defined sense of women's 'wrongs', the unjust sufferings experienced by many women by virtue of their sex. Victoria's complaint against woman's trials— a minor theme in a number of letters to the Princess Royal beginning in 1860—included her belief that a woman's valuable autonomy is compromised even within a successful marriage:

> All marriage is such a lottery—the happiness always an exchange— though it may be a very happy one—still the poor woman is bodily and molly the husband's slave. That always sticks in my throat.

Victoria could hardly be promoted as a feminist icon for today's young women, yet as Thompson concludes, 'If [Victoria] strengthened the moral authority of women in the family rather than making their presence in public life more immediately acceptable, there must have been ways in which the presence of a woman at the head of the state worked at a deeper level to weaken prejudice and make change more possible in the century following her reign.' . . .

Victoria's Independence Emerged Early

At her accession, the diminutive young Queen was often described as pleasingly 'simple' by on-lookers and the press. Indeed, a charming simplicity and modesty of manner, dress, speech and gesture effectively describes the clear-sighted girl who greeted the Archbishop of Canterbury and Lord Conyngham on the morning of June 20th, 1837.

As Britain's 'simple' sweetheart, and thus as unlike her dissolute relations as could be imagined, Victoria at first enjoyed the people's admiration for her freshness and femininity. Yet she expressed her strong will early and often. This characteristic would both support Victoria in times of trial as well as create trouble with her relations. It developed in childhood in part as a response to the political aspirations and machinations of her mother, the Duchess of Kent, and the Duchess's closest advisor, Sir John Conroy. Once she became Queen, Victoria kept the Duchess of Kent at arm's length, while Conroy, after receiving a baronetcy, a payment of 3,000 [pounds sterling] per year and the Grand Cross of the Order of the Bath, was banished from the Queen's presence, though he continued, until 1839, to haunt Buckingham House like a malcontented fairy. Able to please herself by refusing the attentions of those she did not like, Victoria surrounded herself with her favourites—her prime minister, Lord Melbourne, and her former governess, Baroness Louise Lehzen. The protected young monarch was largely unperturbed by working-class unrest such as expressed in the Chartist movement, or by unrelieved suffering in Ireland and squalid areas of London. Victoria wrote to her half-sister, Princess Feodora:

> . . . it is not the splendour of the thing or the being Queen that makes me so happy, it is the pleasant life I lead which causes my peace and happiness.

Yet Victoria was soon roused to outrage when her prime minister was under threat. When Melbourne's Whig government began to fail in May 1839, the Queen faced Melbourne's imminent resignation and the prospect of a (to her mind) disagreeable Tory successor in Sir Robert Peel. Furious at the prospect, Victoria refused to allow the conventional replacement on change of government, of her senior Ladies of the Bedchamber (who were the wives of Whig MPs or peers). The new government was unable to form within this context of sovereign disobedience, and so, to her great satisfaction, though weakened, Melbourne resumed his position. The smug Victoria exulted in a note to Melbourne:

> They wanted to deprive me of my Ladies, and I suppose they would deprive me next of my dressers and my housemaids; they wished to treat me like a girl, but I will show them that I am Queen of England.

Although she could not know it at the time, this event marked the beginning and end of Victoria's successfully-waged legislative obstructions. While in the future she (with Prince Albert) maintained an at times needling presence in government decisions, by September 1841, after a general election in which the Conservatives defeated Melbourne's Liberal (Whig) party, Victoria was forced to accept Peel.

Victoria's Marriage to Prince Albert

The Queen's conduct in the so-called 'Bedchamber Affair' helps to illustrate her fierce loyalty to the many male advisors throughout her life who guided, cajoled and comforted her. The first of these figures was her uncle, King Leopold I of the Belgians (r. 1831–65), the most significant, her husband, Prince Albert, whom she had married on February 10th, 1840. The pain that Victoria felt at the loss of Lord Melbourne (who, following his political demise, suffered a stroke in 1842) as her trusted advisor was eased by the happiness and support she gained through her marriage. After an initial reluctance to consider marriage and a positive dislike of being coerced, Victoria began to lament the lack of young people around her. When Uncle Leopold's choice, her first cousin Prince Albert of Saxe-Coburg-Gotha, and his brother Ernest stopped in England in October, 1839, Victoria, who had found Albert rather dull on their first meeting some three years before, now beheld him with awe: 'Albert is beautiful' she breathed to her journal. Five days later she nervously proposed marriage and was accepted by kisses, embraces and sweet murmurings in German.

Victoria's choice of a young German prince (they were born the same year) was less popular with the press, Tory aristocrats and members of the royal court than with her subjects who gathered to cheer his arrival at Dover a few days before the marriage, and who lined the route of the wedding procession from Buckingham Palace to Windsor Castle where the three-day honeymoon would take place. Cynics insinuated that Albert was a gold-digger. One poet opined:

> He comes the bridegroom of Victoria's choice
> The nominee of Lehzen's Voice;
> He comes to take 'for better or for worse'
> England's fat queen and England's fatter purse.

Although both partners underwent a difficult period of adjustment—Victoria was used to having her own way and lost her temper easily and Albert was homesick and bored with his limited duties and the many official evening events requiring his presence—the marriage was a decided success. The Princess Royal was born within a year of her parents' wedding and eight more children followed; their last child, Princess Beatrice, was born in 1857. Victoria, who suffered from post-natal depression, was not at ease with children—a feeling that had begun as a girl and lasted throughout her life. Less lighthearted in the nursery than her husband, she loved her children, none the less, and greatly preferred their retired familial gatherings and amusements at Osborne House, Balmoral and Windsor Castle, to the exhausting state functions of London life.

The Royal Family's Domestic Influence

During the twenty-year period of Victoria's domestic happiness with Albert, Britain was generally peaceful and increasingly prosperous at home. Victoria's success as Queen was due in large part to the widespread appeal—as both sovereign and 'middle-class' devoted wife and mother embodying the virtues of hard work, charity, practicality and earnestness—she held for a general public also interested in 'home values'. In a long February 1858 letter written to her newly-married eldest daughter, Victoria recounted with pleasure the warm feelings that all classes of people had expressed upon the occasion of Vicky's marriage to Prince Frederick William of Prussia. To the Queen's satisfaction, this kind of support for the Royal Family's affairs demonstrated 'how the people here valued and loved a moral court and a happy domestic home, like, thank God ours has been and is!' The middle classes were energetically elevating trade to respectability and domestic values to a kind of religion. This group, for whom home was a refuge and locus of virtue, were key to this national domestication effort with Victoria at its centre. Victoria was aided to this effect by Albert, of course (whose heightened standing in the government's eyes was clearly signalled by Parliament's passage of the Regency Bill during the Queen's first pregnancy, naming him as sole Regent) and her Tory and Liberal prime ministers (including, Peel, Russell and Palmerston). On the event of her eighteenth wedding anniversary, Victoria boasted in a letter to King Leopold, that her marriage 'has brought . . . universal blessings on this country and Europe!'

Britain's Progress in Industry and Technology

The royal family thus stood as a model at the head of a self-satisfied nation that downplayed internal tensions, while external conflict was used as propaganda to underscore Britain's imperialist ideology of national superiority. The mood was epitomised in the Great Exhibition of the Industry of all Nations at the Crystal Palace in 1851. By promoting the superior talents of both Prince Albert and of British technology, art and commerce, the Great Exhibition united the interests of monarchy, industry and people in celebrating the nation's progress. Over six million visitors flocked to Hyde Park; among these was Charlotte Brontë who commented ". . . it seems as if only magic could have gathered this mass of wealth from all the ends of the earth."

Social Ills During Victoria's Reign

But in spite of what it represented, the Crystal Palace was a 'magical' place in the midst of quotidian urban despair. The 1850 census revealed that London's population had increased by 21 per cent in ten years and now stood at 2,363,000. The cosmopolitan city of theatres, clubs, fashionable shops and modern transportation contrasted with a London of rampant disease, congestion, squalor, crime and poverty. The passage of the Public Health Act of 1848 began to address some of the worst public health problems. The governing classes were unnerved when, in the same year as revolutions broke out on the Continent, some 150,000

Chartist demonstrators marched from Kennington to Westminster with their petition for political representation for labouring men. The Queen classified all such movements as the highest degree of 'disobedience' imaginable: 'Obedience to the laws & to the Sovereign' she told Lord John Russell in August, 1848, 'is obedience to a higher Power.' Yet, as the Chartists' appeal was ultimately peaceful and any instigators of violence punished, Victoria was well satisfied with her subjects' loyalty. Also in 1848, Albert began to visit the south London slums to indicate the royal family's interest in the plight of the lower classes and support for reform measures. . . .

Legislation as well as charitable societies directed toward relieving some social inequalities helped to characterise the Victorian age as one of social activism and reform—much

Queen Victoria

of which was necessary to counteract the effects of a successful Industrial Revolution. The Factory Act of 1844 limited the daily working hours of women and children; the Reform Bill of 1867 completed the general enfranchisement of the middle classes men as well as the majority of male town workers; the Education Act of 1870 acknowledged that the state should support and provide education for children; and the Married Women's Property Bill of 1882 maintained that married women could retain the rights to their property held before or gained during their marriage. In 1897, seventeen different groups formed the National Union of Women's Suffrage Societies (NUWSS) working towards female suffrage as well as other causes pertaining to women's rights.

The Queen's Changing Image

While social reform was a rallying cry for many Victorians who turned their attentions to the world outside the home in an attempt to create a 'home-like' society, the mourning Queen remained inward-looking [after Albert's death in 1861]. But, while duty to the memory of her husband may have governed her days and distracted her from business, Victoria's grief did not mitigate her formidable nature as 'domestic queen'. She maintained tight control over all her households. Those secretaries, servants, and ministers who were able to flatter, amuse and treat her as a woman as well as a monarch were the most successful with her during this period of protracted grief. An ageing Victoria slowly returned to public view, opening Parliament in 1871 and participating—albeit reluctantly—in a celebration of the popular Prince of Wales's recovery from typhoid fever early in the following year. Though she could no longer function as a symbol of domestic happiness, the Queen now represented the more remote, if well-loved, figure of the suffering and patient woman. Victoria's status as 'Our Mother' had begun.

The golden and diamond jubilees (of 1887 and 1897) were wildly successful for Victoria, securing for her a degree of stature hitherto unimagined. No one, including her cheering subjects, expected the Queen to do much at this point in her life—she was simply to represent Britain. Just as at the beginning of her reign when Victoria both benefited and suffered from the image of the girl Queen and the comparisons it generated with male models of monarchy, the image of the grandmother (which she had become, by 1887, thirty times over)—generally an 'invisible' woman of little social power—had to be reinvented to fit Victoria. Although the aged Queen was strictly bound by tradition and a sense of duty, her true nature was rather unlike the severe caricature often promoted: she loved to laugh, enjoyed theatricals, tableaux vivants, and concerts, reading novels and learning some Hindustani from 'the Munshi' (her handsome young Indian servant Abdul Karim). In 1876, the strong-willed Queen, who had pressed for some time for an alteration to her title, was formally declared 'Empress of India'.

Throughout the 1880s, Victoria continued to storm against [Prime Minister William] Gladstone and many of his policies, including Home Rule for Ireland (defeated in 1886), which the Queen felt would damage the union irreparably. In 1886, Victoria would write to a granddaughter that the GOM ('Grand Old Man'), Gladstone, 'behaves abominably. I really think he is cracked.' At the time of her second jubilee, Victoria's name and features were recognisable all over the world; when she died in 1901, few could remember a time when she had not reigned.

Queen Victoria's Legacy

If the Victorian age might be judged an era of optimism, Victoria herself was perhaps its greatest optimist. She held an unshakeable belief in the superiority of all things British (particularly British men). When in late 1899 the elderly Queen was given a report of an especially bad week for the British soldiers fighting in the Boer Wars, she was heard to say, 'Please understand that there is no depression in this house; we are not interested in the possibilities of defeat; they do not exist.' Victoria's strongest personal qualities included dedication, persistence, consistency, health, and loyalty. She acceded to the throne an eighteen-year-old girl, rapidly matured into a young wife and mother, spent long years as a widow and, finally, presided as matriarch over an unwieldy family who would marry into the royal houses of Russia, Germany, Greece, Denmark, Romania, Spain and Norway. Certainly the nature of her monarchy over its sixty-three years reflected these personal life stages and changes. Her political legacy is similarly formidable. While Dorothy Thompson has suggested that 'the fact that [Victoria] was a woman certainly helped to strengthen and stabilise the monarchy, and so to prevent the development in Britain of a more rational republican form of government', it can be argued that her reign initiated the modern monarchy. The historian William M. Kuhn states that in the later years of Victoria's reign, a policy of 'democratic royalism' was in place by which the ceremony and rituals of the monarchy were united with the ideals of democracy to great effect:

> Royal spectacles provided evidence that democracy was rooted in a stable and continuous political tradition . . . They showed how faith, duty, service, and self-sacrifice were necessary to the success of a political system based on consent, trust and a wide degree of active public participation.

Over time, Queen Victoria the historical figure has become 'Victoria'—a cultural artefact and iconic presence open to changing interpretation and reflective of the protean needs and desires of those attempting to understand the zeitgeist of an age through the figure of a powerful woman.

EVENT 8

The Coronation of Queen Victoria:
June 28, 1838

Firsthand Accounts of the Coronation Ceremony

by Christopher Hibbert

Queen Victoria was literally born for the day of her coronation. When, in 1817, it appeared that the British royal family might not have a line of succession, various members of the family took steps to produce heirs. The king's fourth son, Edward, married a German princess, and in 1819, Victoria was born. Although two boys were born after her, her place in the succession preempted any claim they might have to the throne.

Barely eighteen, Victoria ascended the throne of England after an elaborate and lengthy coronation on June 28, 1838. Despite her young age, she was enthusiastic about attending to her duties and being a well-informed monarch. In 1840 she married her German first cousin, Prince Albert, and the couple had nine children in seventeen years. Her children's marriages to a range of European royalty later earned her the title "Grandmother of Europe."

Victoria's reign was marked by social progress and artistic growth. She proved to be an independent and steadfast ruler, continuing her active political life even after being widowed in 1861. She enjoyed a rich life until her death in 1901.

The following excerpt describes Victoria's coronation through

---

Christopher Hibbert, *Queen Victoria: A Personal History*. New York: Basic Books, 2000. Copyright © 2000 by Christopher Hibbert. Reproduced by permission of Basic Books, a member of Perseus Books, LLC.

the comments of various people present for the event, most notably the queen herself. She was a prolific letter writer, and volumes of her correspondence have been published. Writer Christopher Hibbert was allowed access to Victoria's unpublished correspondence, some of which is included in this account of the coronation. Hibbert, a graduate of Oxford University, is the author of numerous biographies of England's historical figures.

After a disturbed night in which she had 'a feeling that something awful was going to happen tomorrow', the Queen was woken up at four o'clock in the morning in her bedroom at Buckingham Palace by the sound of guns in the Park, and 'could not get much sleep afterwards on account of the noise of the people, bands etc. etc.' It was Thursday, 28 June 1838 and she was to be crowned that day in Westminster Abbey. Thousands of people had travelled to London the day before until, as the diarist Mary Frampton told her mother, there were 'stoppages in every street . . . Hundreds of people waiting . . . to get lifts on the railway in vain . . . Not a fly [one-horse carriage] or cab to be had for love or money. Hackney coaches £8 or £12 each, double to foreigners.'

'The uproar, the confusion, the crowd, the noise are indescribable,' Charles Greville [diarist and associate of English royalty] confirmed. 'Horsemen, footmen, carriages squeezed, jammed, intermingled, the pavement blocked up with timbers [for the spectators' stands], hammering and knocking and falling fragments stunning the ears and threatening the head . . . The town all mob, thronging, bustling, gaping and gazing at everything, at anything, or at nothing. The Park one vast encampment, with banners floating on the tops of tents and still the roads are covered, the railroads loaded with arriving multitudes.' He found the racket 'uncommonly tiresome', yet he had to concede that the 'great merit of this Coronation is that so much has been done for the people [the theatres, for example, and many other places of entertainment were to be free that night]. To amuse and interest *them* seems to have been the principal object.'

Preparations for the Event

While not prepared to spend as much as the lavish sum of £243,000 which Parliament had voted for the coronation of King

George IV, the Government were prepared to ensure that the ceremony in the Abbey and its attendant processions and celebrations were conducted with appropriate grandeur and an eye to the enjoyment of the people. £70,000 was deemed a reasonable sum, £20,000 more than had been spent on the coronation of King William IV.

Much attention was paid to the pretty dresses of the Queen's eight young, unmarried trainbearers, the Queen's own three different robes, the new uniforms of the Warders of the Tower and the Yeomen of the Guard, the regalia to be used in the various rites of the Abbey service, and the crown which had been used for the coronation of George IV but which had to be modified for Queen Victoria's much smaller head before being reset with diamonds, pearls, rubies, emeralds and sapphires.

Procession to Westminster Abbey

'It was a fine day,' the Queen, having been up since seven o'clock, wrote in her journal, recalling the long ride to the Abbey in the state coach drawn by eight cream horses, down gravelled streets lined with policemen and soldiers, up Constitution Hill to Hyde Park Corner, then down Piccadilly, St James's and Pall Mall to Trafalgar Square and Whitehall, accompanied by the Duchess of Sutherland, her Mistress of the Robes, and the Earl of Albemarle, the Master of the Horse.

'The crowds of people exceeded what I have ever seen,' the Queen continued her account. 'Many as there were the day I went to the City, it was nothing—nothing to the multitude, the millions of my loyal subjects, who were assembled in *every spot* to witness the Procession. Their good humour and excessive loyalty was beyond everything, and I really cannot say how proud I feel to be the Queen of *such a Nation*. I was alarmed at times for fear that the people would be crushed and squeezed on account of the tremendous rush and pressure.' But she kept smiling and bowing from side to side.

Preceded by the Royal Huntsmen, the Yeomen Prickers and Foresters and the Yeomen of the Guard, and followed by an escort of cavalry, the state coach drew up outside the Abbey door to be greeted by thunderous cheers. Inside the Abbey there were more cheers for the Queen and clapping, too, for Lord Melbourne and for the Duke of Wellington and for Wellington's opponent in the Peninsular War, Marshal Soult, created Duke of Dalmatia by

Napoleon and appointed French Ambassador Extraordinary to the Court of St James's by Louis-Philippe, King of the French. 'Soult was so much cheered, both in and out of the Abbey,' commented the dandiacal merchant, Thomas Raikes, 'that he was completely overcome. He has since publicly said, "*C'est le plus beau jour de ma vie* ["It is the most beautiful day of my life."] It shows that the English believe I have always fought loyally." In the Abbey he seized the arm of his aide-de-camp, quite overpowered, and exclaimed, "This is truly a great people."'

Perceptions of Victoria at Her Coronation

Wellington was predictably not so pleased by his own reception, the 'great shout and clapping of hands'. He looked down the aisle 'with an air of vexation', his friend, Lady Salisbury thought, as if to say, 'This should be for the Queen.' She fully deserved the acclamation, the Duke considered: she carried herself with such charm, dignity and grace, never more so than when the frail and ancient Lord Rolle tripped up as he approached her to make his homage. 'It turned me very sick,' the writer, Harriet Martineau, recorded. 'The large, infirm old man was held by two peers, and had nearly reached the footstool when he slipped through the hands of his supporters, and rolled over and over down the steps, lying at the bottom coiled up in his robes. He was instantly lifted up; and he tried again and again, amidst shouts of admiration of his valour.' 'May I not get up and meet him?' the Queen asked in anxious concern; and, since no one answered her, she outstretched her hand as he manfully rose to his feet and attempted to climb the steps once more as the congregation's vociferous cheers echoed round the Abbey walls.

Wellington's high opinion of the Queen's demeanour was commonly shared. As she caught her first glimpse of the brilliant assembly in the Abbey she was seen to catch her breath and turn pale, clasping her hands in front of her. One of her trainbearers, Lady Wilhelmina Stanhope, believed 'her heart fluttered a little' as they reached the throne; 'at least the colour mounted to her cheeks, brow, and even neck, and her breath came quickly'; and there were those who regarded with some disapproval the smile she exchanged with Baroness Lehzen when, while sitting on the throne, she caught sight of that 'most dear Being' in the box above the royal box.

But to most observers she was a model of dignity and composure as she received the welcome accorded by the boys of Westminster School, whose traditional privilege it was to shout a Latin greeting to the monarch on such occasions. She was equally dignified as she turned from side to side to acknowledge the congregation's shouts of 'God Save Queen Victoria', and as she undertook to 'govern the people of this United Kingdom . . . according to the statutes in Parliament . . . to cause law and justice, in mercy, to be executed in all [her] judgements . . . [and] to maintain the laws of God, the true profession of the Gospel and the Protestant Reformed religion established by law.'

'All this,' she replied to the Archbishop of Canterbury in a clear and steady voice, 'I promise to do.'

She appeared undaunted by the solemnity of the occasion, the blaze of diamonds, the glittering gold plate on the altar, the splendid uniforms of foreign dignitaries, the magnificent robes of the peeresses, the hundreds of faces peering down at her from the specially erected galleries draped with red cloth fringed with gold, and the solemn moment when—as she sat in St Edward's Chair with four Knights of the Garter holding a canopy of cloth of gold over her head—she was anointed by the Archbishop with holy oil, 'as Kings, priests and prophets were anointed'.

She appeared equally composed when the crown was placed upon her head and the peers and peeresses put on their coronets and the bishops their caps to cheers and drum beats, to the notes of trumpets and the firing of guns at the Tower and in the royal parks. Indeed, although in doubt from time to time as to what she was expected to do, she seemed far more calm than the clergy, who, as Charles Greville said, 'were very imperfect in their parts and had neglected to rehearse them'. She was also far calmer than Lord Melbourne who was, she noticed, 'completely overcome and very much affected' when the crown was placed on her head and who, kneeling down to kiss her hand, could not hold back his tears as she 'grasped his with all [her] heart'.

Uncertainty in the Ceremony's Performance

Lord John Thynne, who, as his deputy, took the place of the elderly, infirm Dean of Westminster, admitted that 'there was a continual difficulty and embarrassment, and the Queen never knew what she was to do next'. She whispered to Thynne, who appeared to know more than his colleagues did, 'Pray tell me what to do, for they don't know!' Certainly Edward Maltby, the scholarly, 'remarkably maladroit' Bishop of Durham, who had an important role in the ceremony, never could tell [the Queen], so she complained, 'what was to take place'. At one point he lost his place in the prayer book and began the Litany too soon. When the time came for the ring to be placed on her little finger, the Archbishop endeavoured to place it on her fourth. She told him it was too small; but he persisted, pressing it down so hard that she had 'the greatest difficulty' in getting it off again in the robing room afterwards and had to apply iced water to her fingers for half an hour. When she was given the extremely heavy orb she asked what she was meant to do with it. She was told that she was to carry it; but it then transpired that she had been given it too soon. By this time the Archbishop '(as usual) was so confused and puzzled and knew nothing' that he went away. She, too, was sent away to St Edward's Chapel and had to be summoned back from it when it was discovered that George Henry Law, Lord Ellenborough's brother, the Bishop of Bath and Wells, had turned over two pages at once, thus omitting an essential part of the service.

Nor were the lay peers and trainbearers any more adroit than the clergy. The peers gave the Queen a headache, so her Mistress of the Robes said, by 'very unceremoniously' knocking her crown instead of touching it gently in their act of homage. One of them 'actually clutched hold of' it, while others might well have knocked it off altogether had she not 'guarded herself from any accident or misadventure by having it made to fit her head tightly'. As for the bearers of the Queen's train, they carried it 'very jerkily and badly', one of them admitted, 'never keeping step as she did, even and steadily and with much grace and dignity, the whole length of the Abbey'. Two of them could be heard chattering to each other throughout the service as animatedly as they might have done had they been at a ball. And, when the coronation medals were thrown about in the choir and lower galleries by Lord Surrey, the Treasurer of the Household, everybody scrambled 'with all their might and main to get them, and none more vigorously than the maids-of-honour!'

All in all, Benjamin Disraeli, one of the recently elected Members of Parliament for the borough of Maidstone, told his sister, 'the want of rehearsal' was very obvious: 'Melbourne [who, feeling ill, had dosed himself with laudanum and brandy] looked very awkward and uncouth, with his coronet cocked over his nose, his robes under his feet, and holding the great Sword of State like a butcher . . . The Duchess of Sutherland . . . full of her situation . . . walked, or rather stalked up the Abbey like Juno . . . Lord Lyndhurst [the former and future Lord Chancellor] committed the *faux pas* of not backing from the presence . . . I saw Lord Ward after the ceremony . . . drinking champagne out of a pewter pot, his coronet cocked aside, his robes disordered, and his arms akimbo.'

Nor were Melbourne and Ward the only peers to appear dishevelled in their robes. Indeed, only two of them apparently knew how to wear them properly, both of these being practised performers in amateur theatricals. If Disraeli had gone into St Edward's Chapel—'a small dark place behind the altar', as the Queen described it—he would have seen what Melbourne represented as being 'more *unlike* a Chapel than anything he had ever seen; for, what was called an Altar was covered with sandwiches, bottles of wine, etc.'

A Proud Day for the New Queen

It was almost five hours before the ceremony was over; but conscious that she deserved Lord Melbourne's words of praise—'You did it beautifully—every part of it, with so much taste; it's a thing that you can't give a person advice upon; it must be left to a person'—the Queen did not yet appear to be tired. After an hour spent changing into her purple robe of state in the robing room, then waiting there until half past four, she was taken back through crowds as dense as ever, carrying her sceptre and, heavy as it was, the orb, her close-fitting crown on her head, and the people cheering her all the way to Buckingham Palace where she dashed upstairs to give a bath to her beloved dog, Dash.

After dinner she went into the Duchess of Kent's room; but it was not so much to see her mother—who had burst into tears at the sight of her daughter kneeling alone in the Abbey to receive the Sacrament—as to go out on to the balcony to watch the fireworks in Hyde Park where the next day a grand fair was to be held until the following Monday night. She remained on the balcony until after midnight, when she admitted at last to feeling rather weary. 'You may depend upon it,' Melbourne told her solicitously, 'you are more tired than you think you are.' She herself she decided, would 'ever remember this day as the *proudest*' of her life.

EVENT 9: The Underground Railroad Is Officially Established: 1838

The Underground Railroad Undermined Slavery

by Albert Bushnell Hart

The Underground Railroad is the name given to the network of people, shelters, and transportation by which slaves made their way to freedom from the American North to Canada in the years before the Civil War. Estimates of how many people attained freedom through the Underground Railroad vary widely, but historians agree that tens of thousands of slaves were aided to some degree by the Underground Railroad.

As early as the late eighteenth century, unorganized efforts were made to help slaves escape, but not until the 1830s was an organized system developed. By 1838, the abolitionist movement had taken shape with Robert Purvis as leader of the Underground Railroad. Many of its sympathizers were pacifist Quakers, Covenanters, and Methodists, but countless others were led by an independent sense of morality to participate in the network. Among the most dedicated group of supporters were, not surprisingly, free blacks in the North, such as Josiah Henson, Harriet Tubman, and William Still. The number of people, black and white, involved as "conductors" on the Underground Railroad has been estimated at more than three thousand.

Albert Bushnell Hart, *Slavery and Abolition, 1831–1841*. New York: Harper & Brothers, 1906.

By the end of the Civil War, the Underground Railroad had achieved legendary status, and many of the stories and rumors linked to the organization contain elements of exaggeration. Historians are quick to note that although there was a system in place, an enormous amount of the effort was spontaneous and made possible by luck. They also emphasize that by the time fugitives arrived in the North, they had already survived the most difficult part of the journey. Still, without the support of informed and sympathetic parties in the North, getting all the way to Canada's border would have been exceedingly difficult if not impossible.

In this excerpt, Albert Bushnell Hart, the son and grandson of abolitionists, relates the trials of the fugitive slaves and the workings of the Underground Railroad. Hart was a professor of history at Harvard University and the author of several books about early American history.

The fugitive slaves were surrounded by a host of watchful enemies; unless provided with a forged pass for this occasion, most of them were stopped within ten miles of home and turned back by the patrollers. This danger escaped, every unknown negro found wandering about the country was subject to being taken up and imprisoned, until his captors could advertise him and find his people. If he got clear away from his country or state, he was still far from liberty; he might find his way to some southern town or city and there set up as a freeman, but every negro perfectly knew the danger of recapture under such circumstances, and most of the determined fugitives directed their footsteps north. "We saw the North Star," said Harriet Tubman, "and that told us which way to go." Many escaped by sea; most of the coasters had negro cooks or stewards who could often be induced by sympathy or for a bribe to receive the fugitive and deliver him in a northern port. In the interior, the negro must make his own way from place to place, ignorant of geography and of distance, and chiefly dependent upon the aid of members of his own race: and he found the great belt of wooded mountains stretching from northern Alabama to Pennsylvania a natural highway.

Once across the border, and sometimes before he reached it, the negro entered upon a concealed and intricate system of routes, to which the name "Underground Railroad" was commonly applied.

The term suggests not only a route, but termini, trainmen, and general officials. There was, however, never any general association, hardly so much as a definite understanding between the abolitionists who carried on this forbidden traffic; nor did the conductors and station-masters know all the links in the routes which ran past, or rather into, their doors. The "U.G." can be traced back to informal committees formed in several of the northern cities; and two veterans in this service—[William] Still, in Philadelphia, and the Quaker, Levi Coffin, in Cincinnati—kept a record of the business that went through their stations.

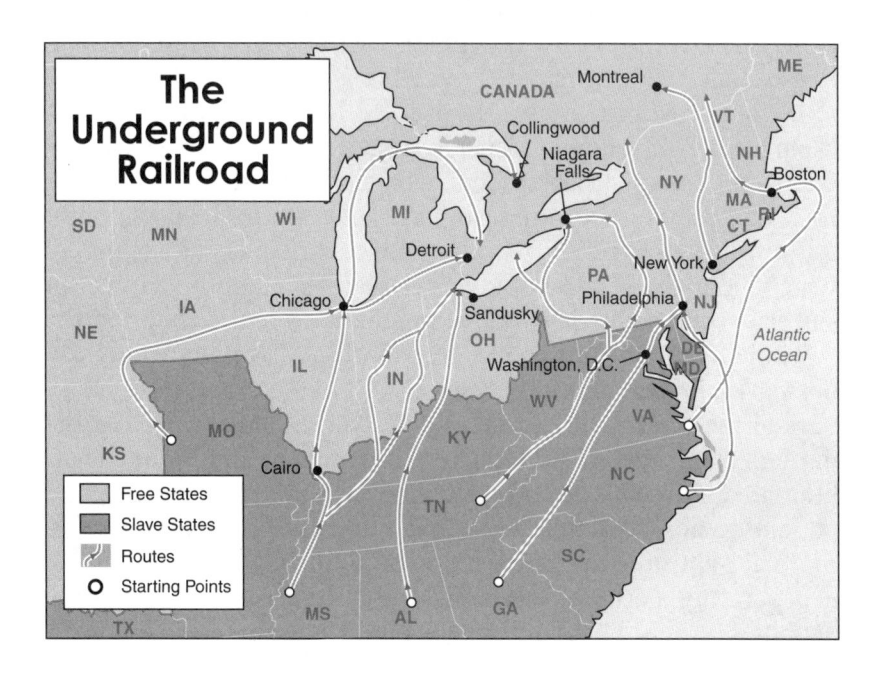

The Underground Railroad had an advertising agency in the understanding, which somehow permeated the slaves in the southern states, that if they once crossed into the free states they would find friends who would forward them from place to place, until they were free from pursuit or arrived at the haven of Canada. To reach these friends every possible method was employed: Henry Box Brown permitted himself to be nailed up in a packing-case and sent by freight to Philadelphia; another hid himself under the guards of a coasting steamer, enduring days of hunger and chill. Ellen Crafts, a very light woman, impersonated a white planter, while her husband played the rôle of personal attendant. As she expected, she was called upon at the Baltimore station to make a written statement as to her companion, but she could not write, and had bound up her arm on the pretence that it was injured. In a few hours they not only escaped, but were entertained as heroes, and their freedom was soon purchased for them. In one instance, three slaves who had some money associated themselves together, hired a travelling coach, bribed a white man to act as their master, and actually drove in state from slavery into freedom.

The Underground Railroad was not a route, but a net-work; not an organization, but a conspiracy of thousands of people banded together for the deliberate purpose of depriving their southern neighbors of their property and of defying the fugitive slave laws of the United States. The geographical area of these operations extended from Maine to Kansas; the routes north of New York began at the seaports and trended towards Canada; in the neighborhood of Philadelphia there was a complexus of routes diverging from two trunk lines, one through Baltimore and the other through Gettysburg. West of the mountains the Underground Railroad was much more flourishing, both because of the hundreds of miles of contiguity between the free and slave states, and because the Ohio River was a highway from one part of the south to another much used by masters and slave-dealers. More than thirty points have been traced on the line of the Ohio and Mississippi rivers where fugitives were received and forwarded. Once on the road, they were carried, commonly at night, by short stages from house to house, concealed during the day, and sent to sure places of refuge.

In some cases the master himself followed; in other cases he "sold his nigger running"—that is, transferred the title to a person, often a professional slavecatcher, who had never seen the slave before, and had no other interest than to get him back and sell him at a profit. This practice, with its cold, commercial calculation, in which there was so little of the patriarchal and dignified aspect of slavery, accented the law—breaking the spirit of the abolitionists.

Though hundreds of people were perfectly well known to harbor slaves, in order to throw suspicion off the scent, younger members of the family, boys or girls, were often employed to drive through the woods with a fugitive. The Underground Railroad was manned chiefly by orderly citizens, members of churches and philanthropical societies. To such law-abiding folk what could be more delightful than the sensation of aiding an oppressed slave, exasperating a cruel master, and at the same time incurring the penalties of defying an unrighteous law? The Underground Railroad furnished the pleasures of a hunt in which the trembling prey was saved from his brutal pursuers; the excitement of a fight in which there was little personal danger; and the joy of the martyr's crown. . . . Hundreds of people deliberately engaged in this work who were not enrolled as abolitionists, and thousands of other people would not lift a hand to help a master recover a slave within a free state. After the British abolition act took effect, in 1840, the soil of Canada became absolutely free, and the British government would not take the slightest pains to assist in returning fugitives. Canada, therefore, was a sure refuge, and many of the routes of the Underground Railroad terminated on the Canadian border or on the Great Lakes, across which there were secret ferries. The nucleus of a negro settlement was made here by an exodus of negroes from Ohio, about 1821, and in Canada West, between Lake Erie and Lake Huron, four or five negro settlements sprang up, to which recruits were sent from cities in the states as well as from the fugitives.

Thousands of Slaves Escaped by the Underground Railroad

The number of persons aided by this system can only be guessed. Official figures in the census of 1850 and 1860 showed a loss of about a thousand slaves a year; but twelve to thirteen hundred a year passed through the Underground Railroad in Ohio alone, and three to four hundred through Philadelphia. In the thirty years from 1830 to 1860, an average of perhaps two thousand slaves a year got away from their masters, of whom perhaps a tenth lost themselves in the south and another tenth got to Canada. This would leave about fifty thousand negroes who, in the fifty years, took to themselves wings and flew away to the free states. As most of the fugitives were grown people, the money loss to the south was, first and last, perhaps thirty million dollars. Nevertheless, it did not seriously affect the value of the slaves except in the border counties of the border states. The Underground Railroad, therefore, was calculated not so much to weaken slavery as to strengthen the antislavery feeling throughout the northern states.

EVENT 9

The Underground Railroad Is Officially Established: 1838

Preface to Records of the Underground Railroad

by William Still

Abolitionist and slave William Still (1821–1902) was born to a large slave family in New Jersey. His father bought his own freedom, and his mother eventually escaped from a Maryland plantation, but Still continued his life as a slave doing farmwork and odd jobs. He became involved in the abolitionist movement in 1847 and rose to a leadership position; in fact, he was instrumental in organizing the Underground Railroad's Philadelphia stop as slaves made their way to Canada. To his delight, he had the opportunity to assist in the escape of one of his brothers. As an organizer and supporter of the Underground Railroad, Still saw how this network of contacts and "stations" made it possible for desperate slaves to realize their dreams of freedom. The growing willingness among slaves to risk extreme danger fueled the abolitionist movement in general and support for the Underground Railroad in particular, and the success of the railroad eroded the institution of slavery in the United States.

Still's commitment to better treatment and equal rights for his fellow black Americans continued for the rest of his life. During the Civil War, Still pursued business opportunities, selling goods to black soldiers and beginning a coal business. During the late 1860s,

---

William Still, *Still's Underground Rail Road Records, Revised Edition, with a Life of the Author, Narrating the Hardships, Hairbreadth Escapes, and Death Struggles of the Slaves in Their Efforts for Freedom, Together with Sketches of Some of the Eminent Friends of Freedom, and Most Liberal Aiders and Advisers of the Road*. Philadelphia: William Still, 1883.

he focused more on African American social issues. He worked to end discrimination on streetcars, assisted an effort to compile information about African Americans, and even played on an all-black baseball team.

In 1872, Still released his recollections of working on the Underground Railroad. His account is one of only a few first-person African American chronicles of such activity written after emancipation. During the nineteenth century, Still's memoirs were the most widely circulated account of the Underground Railroad. As is evident in the Preface that follows, his view of runaway slaves is that they were brave, strong, and right.

Like millions of my race, my mother and father were born slaves, but were not contented to live and die so. My father purchased himself in early manhood by hard toil. Mother saw no way for herself and children to escape the horrors of bondage but by flight. Bravely, with her four little ones, with firm faith in God and an ardent desire to be free, she forsook the prison-house, and succeeded, through the aid of my father, to reach a free State. Here life had to be begun anew. The old familiar slave names had to be changed, and others, for prudential reasons, had to be found. This was not hard work. However, hardly months had passed when the keen scent of the slave-hunters had trailed them to where they had fancied themselves secure. In those days all power was in the hands of the oppressor, and the capture of a slave mother and her children was attended with no great difficulty other than the crushing of freedom in the breast of the victims. Without judge or jury, all were hurried back to wear the yoke again. But back this mother was resolved never to stay. She only wanted another opportunity to again strike for freedom. In a few months after being carried back, with only two of her little ones, she took her heart in her hand and her babes in her arms, and this trial was a success. Freedom was gained, although not without the sad loss of her two older children, whom she had to leave behind. Mother and father were again reunited in freedom, while two of their little boys were in slavery. What to do for them other than weep and pray, were questions unanswerable. For over forty years the mother's heart never knew what it was to be free from anxiety about her lost boys. But no tidings came in answer to her many prayers, until one of them, to the great astonishment of his relatives, turned up in Philadelphia, nearly fifty years of age, seeking his long-lost parents. Being directed to the Anti-Slavery Office for instructions as to the best plan to adopt to find out the whereabouts of his parents, fortunately he fell into the hands of his own brother, the writer, whom he had never heard of before, much less seen or known. And here began revelations connected with this marvellous coincidence, which influenced me, for years previous to Emancipation, to preserve the matter found in the pages of this humble volume.

This Book's Role in Encouraging the Race

And in looking back now over these strange and eventful Providences, in the light of the wonderful changes wrought by Emancipation, I am more and more constrained to believe that the reasons, which years ago led me to aid the bondman and preserve the records of his sufferings, are to-day quite as potent in convincing me that the necessity of the times requires this testimony.

And since the first advent of my book, wherever reviewed or read by leading friends of freedom, the press, or the race more deeply represented by it, the expressions of approval and encouragement have been hearty and unanimous, and the thousands of volumes which have been sold by me, on the subscription plan, with hardly any facilities for the work, makes it obvious that it would, in the hands of a competent publisher, have a wide circulation. And here I may frankly state, that but for the hope I have always cherished that this work would encourage the race in efforts for self-elevation, its publication never would have been undertaken by me.

Freed Slaves Must Work Hard to Elevate States

I believe no more strongly at this moment than I have believed ever since the Proclamation of Emancipation was made by Abraham Lincoln, that as a class, in this country, no small exertion will have to be put forth before the blessings of freedom and knowledge can be fairly enjoyed by this people; and until colored men manage by dint of hard acquisition to enter the ranks of skilled industry, very little substantial respect will be shown them, even with the ballot-box and musket in their hands.

Well-conducted shops and stores; lands acquired and good farms managed in a manner to compete with any other; valuable books produced and published on interesting and important subjects—these are some of the fruits which the race are expected to exhibit from their newly gained privileges.

If it is asked "how?" I answer, "through extraordinary determination and endeavor," such as are demonstrated in hundreds of cases in the pages of this book, in the struggles of men and women to obtain their freedom, education and property.

These facts must never be lost sight of.

The race must not forget the rock from whence they were hewn, nor the pit from whence they were digged.

Like other races, this newly emancipated people will need all the knowledge of their past condition which they can get.

The bondage and deliverance of the children of Israel will never be allowed to sink into oblivion while the world stands.

Those scenes of suffering and martyrdom millions of Christians were called upon to pass through in the days of the Inquisition are still subjects of study, and have unabated interest for all enlightened minds.

The same is true of the history of this country. The struggles of the pioneer fathers are preserved, produced and re-produced, and cherished with undying interest by all Americans, and the day will not arrive while the Republic exists, when these histories will not be found in every library.

The Underground Railroad Reflects the Ongoing Struggle for Freedom in America

While the grand little army of abolitionists was waging its untiring warfare for freedom, prior to the rebellion, no agency encouraged them like the heroism of fugitives. The pulse of the four millions of slaves and their desire for freedom, were better felt through "The Underground Railroad," than through any other channel.

Frederick Douglass, Henry Bibb, Wm. Wells Brown, Rev. J.W. Logan, and others, gave unmistakable evidence that the race had no more eloquent advocates than its own self-emancipated champions.

Every step they took to rid themselves of their fetters, or to gain education, or in pleading the cause of their fellow-bondmen in the lecture-room, or with their pens, met with applause on every hand, and the very argument needed was thus furnished in large measure. In those dark days previous to emancipation, such testimony was indispensable.

The free colored men are as imperatively required now to furnish the same manly testimony in support of the ability of the race to surmount the remaining obstacles growing out of oppression, ignorance, and poverty.

In the political struggles, the hopes of the race have been sadly disappointed. From this direction no great advantage is likely to arise very soon.

Only as desert can be proved by the acquisition of knowledge and the exhibition of high moral character, in examples of economy and a disposition to encourage industrial enterprises, conducted by men of their own ranks, will it be possible to make political progress in the face of the present public sentiment.

Here, therefore, in my judgment is the best possible reason for vigorously pushing the circulation of this humble volume—that it may testify for thousands and tens of thousands, as no other work can do.

WILLIAM STILL, Author.

September, 1878. Philadelphia, Pa.

EVENT 10: Charles Goodyear Discovers the Process of Rubber Vulcanization: 1839

Goodyear's Accomplishment Changes Industry and Everyday Life

by Charles Slack

Charles Goodyear (1800–1860) began his career in the hardware business, first assisting his father, then starting his own firm in Philadelphia. Unfortunately, Goodyear and his father's willingness to extend credit to risky customers led to their businesses' failure. On a visit to New York in 1834, Goodyear happened upon a rubber company, where he saw a valve he thought inferior to one his father made; he saw an opportunity to salvage their ruined financial states by marketing a better product. Although the valve concept did not go far, this event proved to be a crucial turning point in the future inventor's life.

Goodyear learned that there was no good method of processing rubber to withstand heat. After five years of experimentation, he teamed with Nathaniel Hayward, who had discovered that spreading sulfur on rubber prevented it from getting sticky. Goodyear incorporated this knowledge into his most successful process to date and developed rubber vulcanization. Prior to this discovery, rubber was an inferior material because heat rendered it too soft to be useful in machinery. Rubber vulcanization stabilized the material so it would hold its shape and strength under changing temperatures.

Charles Slack, *Noble Obsession: Charles Goodyear, Thomas Hancock, and the Race to Unlock the Greatest Industrial Secret of the Nineteenth Century*. New York: Hyperion, 2002. Copyright © 2002 by Charles Slack. Reproduced by permission of the publisher.

Goodyear spent the next five years perfecting the solutions and processes to achieve the best results with rubber. In 1844, he received his patent for vulcanized rubber.

The uses of vulcanized rubber were, and still are, vast. Vulcanized rubber is used in automobiles, tires, shoes, machinery, medical items, toys, and numerous other objects. The accessibility of rubber that could withstand heat and retain its characteristics changed manufacturing and countless everyday items people use today. Once its profitability became clear, the battle was on to claim Goodyear's patent rights and a bigger share of the market, as Charles Slack explains in the following article.

Slack is a journalist who worked as a reporter in Virginia and Tennessee. As a freelance writer, he has written *Noble Obsession, Blue Fairways*, and *Hetty: The Genius and Madness of America's First Female Tycoon*.

Charles Goodyear's U.S. patent extension lasted for five years after his death. As 1865 approached, the family, led by Charles Jr., decided to attempt one last extension. The patent [for vulcanized rubber] had been under Goodyear's name for two decades, double the protection usually offered to patentees. With each passing year it became more and more difficult to prove that forces beyond the inventor's control had prevented him and his descendants from receiving their just rewards.

The list of licensees was long and impressive; it included the Union India Rubber Company, the Boston Belting Company, Henry Edwards and Partners, the Goodyear Elastic Fabrics Company, the New England Car-Spring Company, the Shoe Associates, Daniel Hodgmen, the New York Rubber Company, the Newark India Rubber Manufacturing Company, Goodyear India Rubber Glove Company, Nashuanneck Manufacturing Company, L. Candee (for "noiseless slate frames"), Nathaniel Hayward, John Haskins, the New York Belting and Packing Company, the New York Rubber Company, and the American Hard Rubber Company (for covering telegraph wire).

Charles Jr. emphasized the destitute relatives, "who are nearly all, if not all, wholly dependent on the settlement of his estate." He further argued his father's aims were always to further the understanding of rubber rather than to reap financial gain: "He carried on his experiments on a very extensive scale in divers places, almost on the scale of a manufacture, for which he never derived any reimbursement or remuneration." As to Goodyear's opus, *Gum-Elastic and Its Varieties*, the son pointed out that the book had never been formally published, that his father never considered the book to have been completed, and printed only a few copies "for his own private use and for the use of his friends. It has never been on sale."

A Dramatic Struggle for the Patent

Opposing the patent extension, Horace H. Day journeyed from New York to Washington for one last chance to harass Charles Goodyear in death as he had in life. By 1865, Day was all but out of the rubber industry, so his interest in the case could have amounted to little more than spite. But he could not contain his innate dislike for Goodyear. Joining Day in opposing the extension was an array of powerful interests whose very presence affirmed the crucial role that rubber was already playing in American industry. One of the loudest unified voices came from the railroads— the Pennsylvania Railroad; the Philadelphia, Wilmington and Baltimore; the Philadelphia and Reading; the Camden and Amboy; and a variety of others who in a few short years had come to rely on vulcanized rubber for belts, packing, car springs, and hose.

Day's attacks against Goodyear at the patent hearing were particularly harsh and spurious. Still clinging to his claim that Goodyear had not invented vulcanization, he accused the dead inventor of having perpetrated a "vast fraud upon the community," and he called him "the great, original confidence man." He claimed absurdly and irrelevantly that Hancock's English patent, since it was issued before Goodyear's American patent, rendered Goodyear's invalid. Without a shred of evidence beyond his own imagination, Day asserted that Goodyear had earned close to five million dollars from the invention, leaving erstwhile investors adrift in poverty while he enjoyed great luxuries: "He has enjoyed all the luxuries which wealth could give; he has in every conceivable way ministered to his vain glory, his appetites and his passions; and, as witnesses tell you, riding through the principal cities in Europe, in the style of nobles and kings; he has squandered money on the right and on the left, wholly indifferent to his moral or legal obligations."

Clarence A. Seward, an attorney for Charles Jr., blasted Day:

"For twenty years and more did he unrelentingly pursue his benefactor. Ordinarily one buried animosity for an enemy in that enemy's grave. Mr. Day seems to be an exception. He has refused to let his wrath go down with the sun."

George Griscom, the lawyer for the opponents of the extension, must have drawn some twitters when he tried to defend Day: "Who can deny that Horace H. Day ranks equal to any man on earth as a thorough-bred, correct and irreproachable merchant, and as an energetic and successful manufacturer?"

The hearings provided some additional comic relief when Day took it upon himself to interrogate Charles Jr. on the witness stand. The son's barely concealed contempt shows through in an exchange that reads like an Abbott and Costello [a comedy duo] routine:

DAY: Name any years in which you worked in India rubber factories, and where.

GOODYEAR: I have worked in India rubber factories in Naugatuck, New Haven, New Brunswick, Newark, Hamden, CT; and also at Providence. I decline to answer as to dates.

DAY: Why do you decline to answer as to dates?

GOODYEAR: I decline to answer.

DAY: When was the first factory erected, to your knowledge, in Naugatuck? State the time as nearly as you can.

GOODYEAR: I decline to answer.

DAY: Do you know?

GOODYEAR: I decline to answer.

DAY: Did you ever reside with your father's family at Springfield, in Massachusetts?

GOODYEAR: I did.

DAY: When?

GOODYEAR: I decline to answer.

DAY: Why do you decline to answer this question when you must see its direct bearing upon the question of the knowledge necessary to enable you to fairly present your father's case before Congress?

GOODYEAR: I decline to answer.

The exchange must have warmed the hearts of the Goodyear contingent—the inventor's son, with Bartleby-like indifference, rebuffing questions put to him by the arrogant, white-maned, and increasingly red-faced Day. In the end, though, the cause of the heirs was doomed, not by Day's machinations, nor even the powerful forces against the extension, but by the patent office's reluctance to extend a patent that had already been held for twenty years. The patent office refused the request, announcing that Charles Goodyear's patent for vulcanized rubber would expire on June 15, 1865. The invention that he had always seen as his gift (or, rather, God's through him) would now be, in the truest sense, just that. Vulcanized rubber belonged to everybody. . . .

Worldwide Impact of Rubber Industry

In 1861, the year after Goodyear died, Union armies marched off to battle wearing rubber ponchos and pitching rubber tents to protect themselves from the elements. Battlefield doctors carried rubber medicine bottles and soldiers carried rubber powder flasks. By the late 1800s, a material once forgotten was vital enough to drive mild-mannered dentists to murder. On Easter Sunday, 1879, Josiah Bacon, treasurer of the Goodyear Dental Vulcanite Company, was found dead in his San Francisco hotel room. The company—unrelated to the Goodyear family—owned the patent for hard rubber dentures, which had revolutionized the dental industry by replacing ill-fitting wooden dentures with snug rubber. Prompted by Bacon's bulldog tactics, the Goodyear Dental Vulcanite Company exacted usurious fees from dentists across the country and zealously tracked down and prosecuted any and all who violated the patent. Dentists claimed they had no choice but to violate it—patients demanded vulcanite, but dentists could not afford the steep fees. In a fit of anger Dr. Samuel P. Chalfant, a defendant in one of Bacon's lawsuits, tracked the treasurer down and assassinated him. Chalfant served ten years in prison before being released. He continued his practice, and to this day remains something of a hero in the dental community.

Vulcanization created a worldwide demand for South American rubber. What had once been a sleepy trade of a material in little demand now created vast fortunes for some and torment and abuse for thousands of others. Grandiose opera houses sprouted in Brazilian jungle towns such as Manaus, along with saloons where the finest French champagne could be bought at four in the morning. The Brazilian rubber boom ended almost as suddenly as it began, when an English adventurer named Henry A. Wickham spirited away seventy thousand *Hevea brasiliensis* seeds from Brazil. The seeds were planted in Kew Gardens, outside of London. Some two thousand seedlings were then transported to the Far East. The move created the plantation rubber industry in Asia and in one stroke effectively killed the Brazilian rubber industry.

By the dawn of World War II, rubber was so important that Japanese control of Far Eastern plantations threatened the Allied war effort. Rubber was needed for vehicle and airplane tires, rubber rafts, and rubber lining for gas tanks, to seal bullet holes. It was used for boots and boats and pontoon bridges. The United States led a massive effort to create a usable synthetic rubber. By the end of the war, synthetic rubber was well on its way to overshadowing natural rubber. And yet every ounce of synthetic rubber still had to be vulcanized in much the same way as pioneered by Charles Goodyear.

Goodyear's Descendants

Goodyear's name lived on in the rubber industry because of the many licensees that adopted it. A casual observer would have assumed a family dynasty in the making, but Goodyear's descendants had little to do with any of it, and received little financial reward. Charles Jr. had assisted his father in life and was charged with the unenviable task of straightening out his estate after his death. But he dropped out of the rubber business not long after his father died. He would make his mark as an inventor in the shoe industry. He developed the Goodyear Welt, a mechanized method for fixing the upper shoe to the sole that is still widely used today. The shoes I am wearing as I write say "100% Caoutchouc" (the old name for rubber) on the outer sole and "Goodyear Welt" on the insole, a moving if unintended tribute to the combined talents of father and son.

Another son, William Henry, grew up to became a renowned art historian, author of several influential books, and curator at the Metropolitan Museum of Art in New York and the Brooklyn Institute Museum. The Goodyear invention streak would take a final, odd twist with granddaughter Anna Goodyear, a severe-looking woman who ran a mission in Boston's North End. In 1907 Anna devised a spanking machine for adult criminals. The rotating platform could be adjusted to the height of the offender, and set for one to fifty blows. Anna insisted the humiliation of a public spanking would be more effective than imprisonment in rehabilitating offenders. She offered to present a free machine to any town or city that wanted one, but there were few takers, even at such a reasonable price.

The force that did more than any other to advance Goodyear's name and cement it to his invention in the public mind had no formal connection with the man or his family. Frank Seiberling of Akron, Ohio, born a year before Goodyear's death, had spent twenty years in various enterprises, including a twine and cordage factory, mills, and a streetcar company. Nearly wiped out in a national financial panic started by the failure of the Philadelphia and Reading Railroad, Seiberling by 1898 was looking for a new opportunity. He scraped together the down payment for a defunct Akron factory on twelve acres without knowing what exactly he would manufacture.

Bicycles were hugely popular, and a new horseless carriage seemed promising. Akron was already home to two established rubber manufacturers, Diamond Rubber Company and B.F. Goodrich. Perhaps the growing city could support one more. Seiberling's brother, Charles, joined him in the venture. Instead of naming the company after themselves, the brothers selected Goodyear's name, to honor, they said, the inventor's perseverance and dedication. The name also had an agreeable similarity to the more established Goodrich company. The Goodyear Tire & Rubber Company opened its doors November 21, 1898, with thirteen employees.

As Goodyear Tire & Rubber grew into the world's largest tire company, a true manufacturing colossus, the relationship between the company and its namesake remained a peculiar one. Many companies have dealt with a legacy of eccentric founders. But few have been so closely associated with a man who was *not* the founder. To this day most people assume a direct connection between Charles Goodyear and the tire company, an assumption that generally works to the favor of both.

Because of its name, the company over the years has become the heir to Goodyear lore and memorabilia. The somewhat threadbare World of Rubber exhibit, located on the fourth floor of Goodyear Hall in Akron, features a mockup of a shack where a life-size Charles Goodyear toils at his invention over a potbellied stove. Nearby are glass cases exhibiting various medals awarded Goodyear, some manuscripts, buttons, combs, and other objects the inventor fashioned out of hard rubber, portraits on hard rubber by [painter George P.A.] Healy, and other items.

A bronze statue of Charles Goodyear, unveiled during the company's massive celebration of the hundredth anniversary of vulcanization, still gazes over Akron from its leafy perch in a downtown park. In a rather bizarre bit of self-congratulation during a company dinner in 1925, top executives watched Goodyear return from the grave (as projected through a company flack). He told them: "I have come back tonight to visit the great structure that you have erected in my name. I have come back in pride—because you have not belied your heritage, because you have pursued the goal of service to mankind, because you have been unafraid, because you have the faith to move mountains."

Over the years, the company has walked a fine line between embracing the Goodyear legacy and making it clear that there is no *legal* connection between the firm and the inventor or his family. Indeed, none of Goodyear's descendants have ever had a prominent position in the company. The company was given to acts of generosity with some descendants. When grandson Charles Goodyear III and granddaughter Clara Goodyear (married cousins) fell on hard times during the 1930s, the company quietly arranged for a monthly stipend of one hundred dollars per month, later doubled, for the rest of their lives. At other times, the company strove to keep relations at arm's length. Granddaughter Rosalie Eliot Heaton, irked when the company refused to buy a pair of rubber cuff buttons worn by Goodyear at the court of Napoléon III, began writing angry public letters to company directors. "Grandfather's life was faithful, just and righteous," she wrote. "But our family has had no evidence of concrete tribute being paid to us either for Goodyear's name or process which has been used for some sixty years."

Whatever Goodyear descendants have thought of the connection, it is difficult to imagine Charles himself being anything but pleased. He would have been gratified to see his name on millions of vehicle tires. Especially, though, the aesthete in him would have loved the blimp that carries the Goodyear name to sporting events around the country. A man who always saw his quest as a holy mission would have adored seeing his name hovering godlike over great stadiums, where thousands of rubber-soled spectators gather to watch grown men and women play games with balls made of vulcanized rubber.

CHRONOLOGY

1820
Missouri Compromise maintains balance between slave states and free states in the Union; Maine is admitted to the Union; publication of English poet Percy Bysshe Shelley's *Prometheus Unbound*.

1821
Michael Faraday discovers electromagnetic rotation; Guatemala, Panama, and Santo Domingo declare their independence from Spain; Missouri is admitted to the Union; Mexico gains independence from Spain; the first college for women in the United States opens in Waterford, NY; death of English poet John Keats; death of exiled Napoléon Bonaparte; birth of Russian novelist Fyodor Dostoyevsky.

1822
Liberia is founded as a colony for free slaves from the United States; Brazil wins independence from Portugal; the lengthy and bloody Ashanti War begins in West Africa; death of Shelley; birth of genetics pioneer Gregor Mendel; birth of French scientist Louis Pasteur.

1823
Monroe Doctrine enunciates America's opposition to European intervention in the Western Hemisphere; France intervenes in Spanish Revolution to defeat rebels and restore King Ferdinand VII to the throne; Pope Leo XII succeeds Pope Pius VII.

1824
German composer Ludwig von Beethoven completes his *Ninth Symphony*; the Bureau of Indian Affairs is established in the United States; death of English poet George Gordon, Lord Byron; Simon Bolívar liberates Peru and becomes president; outbreak of the first Anglo-Burmese War.

1825
Opening of the Erie Canal in upstate New York; precedent-setting Decembrist uprising in Russia; John Quincy Adams is elected president of the United States; birth of Austrian composer Johann Strauss.

1826
Deaths, unrelated, of American statesmen and presidents John Adams and Thomas Jefferson, both on July 4; publication of James Fenimore Cooper's *The Last of the Mohicans;* cholera epidemic sweeps India.

1827
Death of Ludwig van Beethoven; publication of John James Audubon's *Birds of America;* death of English poet and engraver William Blake.

1828
Publication of Noah Webster's *American Dictionary of the English Language;* birth of Russian novelist Leo Tolstoy; Uruguay gains independence as a result of a peace treaty between Brazil and Argentina.

1829
Andrew Jackson is elected president of the United States; first passenger railroad in the United States opens; Jackson introduces spoils system; first National Negro Convention assembles in Philadelphia.

1830
Joseph Smith founds Church of Jesus Christ of Latter-day Saints (Mormonism); Indian Removal Act authorizes federal government to relocate Native American tribes to lands of the government's choosing; birth of American poet Emily Dickinson; July Revolution in Paris; Belgium gains its independence from the Netherlands.

1831
Nat Turner uprising; Leopold I becomes king of the Belgians; publication of Victor Hugo's *The Hunchback of Notre Dame;*

cholera epidemic reaches central Europe from Russia; London Bridge is opened for traffic; British naturalist Charles Darwin embarks on his groundbreaking oceanographic voyage aboard the HMS *Beagle*, a journey that will inform his theory of evolution; Jamaican slaves are emancipated.

1832
Treaty of London for Greek independence; birth of English novelist Lewis Carroll; Oregon Trail becomes the chief route for settlers heading to the American West; New England Anti-Slavery Society is established; Black Hawk War erupts as the U.S. Army is summoned to suppress tribal resistance to resettlement.

1833
Slavery is abolished throughout the British Empire; Factory Act in England prohibits child labor; establishment of the Boston Academy of Music, America's first music school; birth of German composer Johannes Brahms; the first steamship to cross the Atlantic Ocean under its own power begins its historic journey.

1834
Death of English poet and philosopher Samuel Taylor Coleridge; English inventor Charles Babbage designs an analytical machine that is a precursor of the modern computer; Spanish Inquisition officially ends after more than 350 years.

1835
Publication (in France) of Alexis de Tocqueville's *Democracy in America;* American author Mark Twain (Samuel Clemens) is born; Boers (Dutch settlers in South Africa) begin their Great Trek north to gain freedom from British control; an earthquake in Chile destroys a city and leaves five thousand dead; P.T. Barnum begins first circus tour of the United States; publication of Hans Christian Andersen's first book of fairy tales.

1836
In March, Texan defenders are utterly defeated at the battle of the Alamo; one month later Texans overcome Antonio López de Santa Anna and his Mexican forces at the Battle of San Jacinto, bringing about Texas's independence; Arkansas admitted to the Union.

1837
Martin Van Buren is elected president of the United States; Michigan admitted to the Union; publication of Charles Dickens's *Oliver Twist*.

1838
Underground Railroad begins; Amistad slave mutiny; Cherokee Trail of Tears to Oklahoma; smallpox epidemic in England; Frederick Douglass escapes slavery; London's National Gallery opens on Trafalgar Square; coronation of Queen Victoria of England.

1839
American inventor Charles Goodyear discovers process of rubber vulcanization; Louis J.M. Daguerre develops the first daguerreotype photograph; first bicycle built in Scotland by Kirkpatrick Macmillan; birth of French painter Paul Cézanne; First Opium War erupts between China and Britain; London Treaty is signed, guaranteeing Belgian neutrality.

FOR FURTHER RESEARCH

Books

Robert Greenhalgh Albion and Jennie Barnes Pope, *The Rise of New York Port: 1815–1860*. New York: C. Scribner's Sons, 1939.

Alejandro Alvarez, *The Monroe Doctrine: Its Importance in the International Life of the State of the New World*. New York: Oxford University Press, 1924.

Timothy E. Anna, *Forging Mexico: 1821–1835*. Lincoln: University of Nebraska Press, 1998.

Noel Annan et al., *Ideas and Beliefs of the Victorians: An Historic Revaluation of the Victorian Age*. London: Sylvan, 1949.

Herbert Aptheker, *American Negro Slave Revolts*. New York: International, 1974.

C.W. Crawley, *The Question of Greek Independence: A Study of British Policy in the Near East, 1821–1833*. Cambridge, UK: Cambridge University Press, 1930.

Douglas Dakin and Edward S. Forster, *A Short History of Modern Greece, 1821–1956*. London: Methuen, 1958.

Dwight Lowell Dumond, *The Crusade for Freedom in America*. Ann Arbor: University of Michigan Press, 1961.

Philip S. Foner and Robert James Branham, eds., *Lift Every Voice: African American Oratory, 1787–1900*. Tuscaloosa: University of Alabama Press, 1998.

Yekutiel Gershoni, *Black Colonialism: The Americo-Liberian Scramble for the Hinterland*. Boulder, CO: Westview, 1985.

Albert Bushnell Hart, *Slavery and Abolition, 1831–1841*. New York: Harper & Brothers, 1906.

Christopher Hibbert, *Queen Victoria: A Personal History.* New York: Basic Books, 2000.

Burton Kirkwood, *The History of Mexico.* Westport, CT: Greenwood, 2000.

Keith J. Laidler, *To Light Such a Candle: Chapters in the History of Science and Technology.* Oxford, UK: Oxford University Press, 1998.

Richard W. Leopold, *The Growth of American Foreign Policy: A History.* New York: Knopf, 1962.

Anatole G. Mazour, *Russia: Past and Present.* New York: Van Nostrand, 1951.

Robert L. Millett and Joseph Smith, *Joseph Smith: Selected Sermons & Writings.* New York: Paulist, 1989.

Augustus Oakes and R.B. Mowat, eds., "Independence of Greece," *The Great European Treaties of the Nineteenth Century.* Oxford, UK: Clarendon, 1918.

Louis Ruchames, *The Abolitionists: A Collection of Their Writing.* New York: Putnam, 1963.

Edith Sitwell, *Victoria of England.* Boston: Houghton Mifflin, 1936.

Charles Slack, *Noble Obsession: Charles Goodyear, Thomas Hancock, and the Race to Unlock the Greatest Industrial Secret of the Nineteenth Century.* New York: Hyperion, 2002.

William Still, *Still's Underground Rail Road Records, Revised Edition, with a Life of the Author, Narrating the Hardships, Hairbreadth Escapes, and Death Struggles of the Slaves in Their Efforts for Freedom, Together with Sketches of Some of the Eminent Friends of Freedom, and Most Liberal Aiders and Advisers of the Road.* Philadelphia: William Still, 1883.

Henry David Thoreau, *The Major Essays of Henry David Thoreau.* Ed. Richard Dillman. Albany, NY: Whitson, 2001.

Nat Turner and Thomas Gray (interviewer), "The Confessions of Nat Turner, the Leader of the Late Insurrection in Southampton, VA," Yuval Taylor, ed., *I Was Born a Slave: An Anthology of Classic Slave Narratives.* 2 vols. Chicago: Lawrence Hill, 1999.

Charles Morrow Wilson, *Liberia.* New York: W. Sloane, 1947.

Periodicals

Vera Borokova, "The Decembrists, 170 Years Later," *Russian Life*, vol. 38, no. 6, December 1995.

Richard R. Flores, "Memory-Place, Meaning and the Alamo," *American Literary History*, vol. 10, no. 3, 1998.

John MacKenzie, "The Victorian Vision: Inventing New Britain," *History Today*, April 2001.

Bjorn Wittrock, "One, None, or Many? European Origins and Modernity as a Global Condition," *Daedalus*, vol. 129, no. 1, 2000.

INDEX

abolition, 61, 113, 117, 118
Adams, John Quincy, 40–41, 43–44
Africa
  cultural and historical legacy of, 32–33
  differences among Africans in, 34–35
  see also Liberia
African Americans
  in Liberia, 30–31
  American race relations and, 33
  self-image of, 33–34
  Underground Railroad and, 113–17, 118–22
  see also Nat Turner Uprising, aftermath
agriculture, in Liberia, 35–36
Albert (prince of Saxe-Coburg-Gotha), 100–101, 103–104, 106
Alexander I (czar of Russia), 12, 55–56, 87, 88
alternating current, 20
American Colonization Society, 28
Ampère, André Marie, 16, 17
Anglo-French Treaty of Whitehall, 39–40
Aptheker, Herbert, 61
Argentina, 44
Army of the Three Guarantees, 26
Austria, 11–12

Bacon, Josiah, 127
balance-of-power theory, 45
Battle of Navarino, 89–90

Beatrice (princess of Great Britain), 101
Belize, 44, 46
benzene, 15, 19
B.F. Goodrich, 129
Bonaparte, Joseph, 22
Brazil, 43, 127–28
Brontë, Charlotte, 102
Brown, Henry Box, 115
Burnside, Ambrose E., 47

Cádiz junta, 22
California, 44–45
Canada, 115–17
Canning, George, 88, 89, 90
Capodistrias, Ioánnis Antónias, 91
Catholic Church
  in Greece, 86
  in Mexico, 23, 26
Chalfant, Samuel P., 127
Chartists, 103
clathrate compound, 16
Clay, Henry, 43–44
Clayton-Bulwer Treaty, 47
Cobb, Jeremiah, 67
Codrington, Edward, 90
Coffin, Levi, 115
colonization. See Monroe Doctrine
Congress of Vienna, 85
Congress on Africa, 28
Conroy, John, 99
Coräes, Adamantos, 86–87
Corelli, Marie, 98
Crafts, Ellen, 115–16
Crawley, C.W., 12
Creoles, 24, 26, 27

INDEX 139

Crystal Palace, 102–103
Cuba, 40–41

Dalmatia, Duke of. *See* Soult, Marshal
Day, Horace H., 125–27
Decembrist revolt, 12–13, 55–60
"democratic royalism," 105
Diamond Rubber Company, 129
Disraeli, Benjamin, 111–12
Dominican Republic, 46
Drewry, W.S., 63, 64, 66
dynamo, 20

Edwards, Amelia B., 34
1812 constitution (Mexico), 25
1827 Treaty of London, 89
1832 Treaty of London, 90–91
  terms of, 91–92
  text of, 92–96
electrical energy, 16–17
electromagnetic induction, 10, 14, 17–20
electromagnetic rotation, 14, 19
electromagnetism, 15–16
Emancipation Proclamation, 120
energy, 14, 15
  see also electromagnetic induction
England
  Greece and, 11–12, 88–89
  Monroe Doctrine and, 41–42, 44–45, 47, 52–54
  political separation of U.S. from, 38
Europe
  influence of, in the Americas, 10–11
  New World colonization by, 40–41
  support for Greek independence by, 88–89
  see also individual names of countries

Factory Act of 1844, 103
Falkland Islands, 44, 46
Faraday, Michael, 10, 14–15
  electrical energy discovery by, 16–17
  electromagnetic induction discovery by, 17–18
  legacy of, 19–20
  as physicist, 15–16
  work habits of, 18–19
feminism, 98–99, 103
Ferdinand VII (king of Spain), 10, 24, 25
Fish, Hamilton, 47
Florida, 40–41
Floyd, John, 65, 67, 68
foreign policy, of United States. *See* Monroe Doctrine
Frampton, Mary, 107
France
  Creoles and, 24
  1832 Treaty of London and, 90–96
  Greece and, 11–12
  Monroe Doctrine and, 41–42, 43–44, 46, 48
Francis, Salathul, 77–78
Frederick William (prince of Prussia), 101
Frelinghuysen, Frederick T., 47

Garibay, Pedro de, 25
Garrison, William Lloyd, 63
George IV (king of England), 108
Gladstone, William, 104
Goodyear, Anna, 128–29
Goodyear, Charles, Jr., 124–27, 128
Goodyear, Charles, Sr., 123–24
  descendants of, 128–29
  impact of, on rubber industry, 127–28
  legacy of, 129–31

patents of, 124–27
see also Goodyear Tire &
  Rubber Company
Goodyear, Charles, III, 130
Goodyear, Clara, 130
Goodyear, William Henry, 128
Goodyear Dental Vulcanite
  Company, 127
Goodyear Tire & Rubber
  Company, 129–30
Goodyear Welt, 128
Grant, Ulysses, 47
Gray, Thomas, 73
Great Britain. *See* England
Great Exhibition of the Industry
  of All Nations, 102
Greece
  independence of, 84–96
    Battle of Navarino and, 89–90
    early revolution and, 87–88
    1832 Treaty of London and,
      90–96
    European influence and,
      88–89
    historical events leading to,
      85–86
    Turkish rule and, 86–87
    War of Independence and,
      11–12, 85
  Monroe Doctrine and, 43
  see also Hellenism
Greville, Charles, 107, 110
Griscom, George, 126
Guerrero, Vicente, 26
Guizot, Francois, 45
Gum-Elastic and Its Varieties
  (Charles Goodyear Jr.), 125

Hark (slave), 75, 76, 82
Hart, Albert Bushnell, 113
Hayward, Nathaniel, 123, 124
Heaton, Rosalie Eliot, 130
Hellenism, 86
Henry, Joseph, 17, 20

Henry (slave), 75, 76, 82
Henson, Josiah, 113
Hetaeria Philikë, 87
Hevea brasiliensis, 128
Hibbert, Christopher, 106
Hidalgo y Costilla, Miguel, 24
Hudson's Bay Company, 44
Humboldt, Alexander von, 24

Ibrahim Pasha, 88, 90
Industrial Revolution, 103
intellectualism, 57
isolationism, 40
Iturbide, Augustin, 26–27
Iturrigaray, José de, 24–25

Jackson, Andrew, 44
Jefferson, Thomas, 40–41

Kent, Duchess of, 99, 112
Kirkwood, Burton, 21
Kuhn, William M., 105

labor
  in England, 103
  in Liberia, 35–36
Ladies of the Bedchamber, 100
Laidler, Keith J., 14
land grants, in Liberia, 35
Law, George Henry, 111
Lehzen, Louise, 99
Leopold, Richard W., 38
Leopold I (king of Belgium), 91,
  102
Liberia, 28–30, 71
  African Americans in, 30–31
  African culture and history in,
    32–33
  government and economy in, 30
  map of, 31
Lincoln, Abraham, 47, 120
Lynch, John, 22

Madison, James, 41

INDEX 141

magnetism, 16–17
   see also electrical energy
Maltby, Edward, 111
Martineau, Harriet, 109
Maryland, 70–71
Maryland State Colonization
   Society, 71
Maxwell, James Clerk, 15, 19
mayorazgo, 23
Mazour, Anatole G., 55
mechanical energy, 14–17
Melbourne, Lord, 99–100, 108,
   110, 111–12
Mexicanidad, 22
Mexico, 21–22
   conflict among peoples of,
      24–25
   financial relationship with
      Spain, 22–24
   Monroe Doctrine and, 44–45,
      46, 48
   political upheaval in, 25–27
*Mexico: The Struggle for Peace
   and Bread* (Tannenbaum), 25
Miliukov, Paul N., 59
Monroe, James, 38, 49
   see also Monroe Doctrine
Monroe Doctrine, 38–39
   in 1830s and 1840s, 44–45
   in 1850s and 1860s, 45–47
   in 1870s and 1880s, 47–48
   on European authority, 42–43
   historical background of, 39–41
   interpretation and application
      of, 43–44
   reasons for, 41–42
   text of, 50–54
Moore, Putnam, 63
motors, electric, 19–20
Mowat, R.B., 84

Napoléon Bonaparte. *See*
   Napoléon I
Napoléon I, 10, 12, 57

Napoleonic Wars, 12, 56, 87
Nat Turner Uprising, 61–62
   aftermath of, 67–72
   capture of Turner and, 67
   death toll from, 66–67, 76–79
   events during, 65–66
   location of, 62–63
   suppression of rebellion
      following, 70–72
Nelson (slave), 75, 82
Nicholas I (czar of Russia),
   12–13, 56, 59–60, 88–90
Nobel Prize, 19
Northern Society, 58
no-transfer policy, 40–41, 47

Oakes, Augustus, 84
Odessa, 86
Oersted, Hans Christian, 16, 17,
   18
Oregon, 44–45
Otho (king of Greece), 93–96
Ottoman Empire, 11
   see also Turkey

Panama Canal, 47
Passing of the Great Queen, The
   (Corelli), 98
patents, for rubber, 124–27
Peel, Robert, 100
Peete, Alexander P., 80
Peninsulares, 24, 26, 27
Peter the Great (czar of Russia),
   55
Phanariot Greeks, 86
Phillips, Richard, 16
Phipps, Benjamin, 67, 82–83
Pixii, Hyppolyte, 20
Plan de Iguala, 26
Polk, James K., 45
Portugal, 10, 11, 43, 50–52
Powell, G.W., 67
principle, of self-excitation, 20
Public Health Act of 1848, 102

Pugachev, 57
Purvis, Robert, 113

race relations. *See* Nat Turner
  Uprising; Underground
  Railroad
racial pride, 33–37
Raikes, Thomas, 109
railroads, rubber and, 125
Randolph, John, 43
Reforma, 27
Regency Bill, 102
Reigo, Rafael de, 10, 25
Richmond Compiler (newspaper),
  65, 69
Richmond Enquirer (newspaper),
  63, 68
Richmond Whig (newspaper), 66
Ritchie, Thomas, 72
Roatán, 44, 46
Rolle, Lord, 109
rotary electric generator, 20
Rothschild, Emma, 13
Royal Law of Consolidation,
  23–24
rubber
  industry, 127–31
  patents, 124–27
  vulcanization, 123–24
Ruffin, Thomas, 67
Rush, Richard, 40
Russell, John, 103
Russia
  Decembrist revolt and, 12–13,
    55–60
  1832 Treaty of London and,
    90–96
  Greece and, 12, 89
  Monroe Doctrine and, 41–42,
    49–52

Sam (slave), 75, 82
secret societies
  in Greece, 87

  in Russia, 57–59
serfdom, 58
Seward, Clarence A., 125–26
Seward, William H., 46, 47
shoe industry, 128
Sieberling, Charles, 129
Sieberling, Frank, 129
Siemens, Werner von, 20
Slack, Charles, 123
slavecatchers, 116, 119
slavery
  beginning of antislavery
    movement and, 72
  founding of Liberia and, 28, 31
  Underground Railroad and,
    113–17, 118–22
  see also Nat Turner Uprising
Smyth, John H., 28
Soult, Marshal, 108–109
Southampton, Virginia, 62–63
Southern Society, 58
Spain, 10–11
  financial relationship with
    Mexico and, 22–24
  Monroe Doctrine and, 40–44,
    46, 49–52
Stanhope, Wilhelmina, 109
Still, William, 113, 118
  record keeping by, 115
  on Underground Railroad,
    118–22
Sturgeon, William, 18, 20

Tannenbaum, Frank, 25
Texas, 44
Thompson, Dorothy, 98, 105
Thousand Miles up the Nile, A
  (Edwards), 34
Thynne, John, 110–11
transformers, electrical, 20
Travis, Joseph, 61, 63, 65, 73, 76
Tubman, Harriet, 113
Turkey, 11–12, 86–87, 89–90
Turner, Benjamin, 63, 74

Turner, Nat, 68, 73
  background and personality of, 63–64, 74
  capture and execution of, 67, 81–83
  on events of uprising, 76–80
  on his childhood, 74
  leadership of, 75
  plans of, for uprising, 75–76
  religious influence of, 63–65, 74
  revolt planned by, 64–65, 75–76
  see also Nat Turner Uprising

Underground Railroad, 113–14
  map of, 115
  operation of, 113–17
  records, 118–22
Union of Salvation, 58
United Slavs, 58

Vallone, Lynne, 97
Varley, C.F., 20
Venezuela, 54
Victoria (queen of England), 10, 97, 101, 106–107
  British industry and technology and, 102
  coronation of, 106–12
  domestic influence of royal family and, 101–102
  as Empress of India, 104
  image of, 103–104
  independence of, 99–100
  legacy of, 104–105
  marriage of, 100–101
  social ills during reign of, 102–103
  on women's roles, 98–99
Virginia, 70–72
vulcanization, 123–24

War of Independence (Greece), 12, 85
Welfare Society, 58
Wellington, Duke of, 89, 90, 108
Westminster Abbey, 108–12
Whitehead, Margaret, 78
Whitehead, Richard, 78
Wickham, Henry A., 128
William IV (king of England), 108
Will (slave), 76

Yermo, Gabriel de, 25
Ypsilanti, Alexander, 87